Culturally Responsive
Data Literacy

Ellen B. Mandinach
WestEd

ROWMAN & LITTLEFIELD
Lanham • Boulder • New York • London

Acquisitions Editor: Nathan Davidson
Acquisitions Assistant: Hollis Peterson
Sales and Marketing Inquiries: textbooks@rowman.com

Credits and acknowledgments for material borrowed from other sources, and reproduced with permission, appear on the appropriate pages within the text.

Published by Rowman & Littlefield
An imprint of The Rowman & Littlefield Publishing Group, Inc.
4501 Forbes Boulevard, Suite 200, Lanham, Maryland 20706
www.rowman.com

86-90 Paul Street, London EC2A 4NE

Copyright © 2025 by Ellen B. Mandinach

All rights reserved. No part of this book may be reproduced in any form or by any electronic or mechanical means, including information storage and retrieval systems, without written permission from the publisher, except by a reviewer who may quote passages in a review.

British Library Cataloguing in Publication Information Available

Library of Congress Cataloging-in-Publication Data

Names: Mandinach, Ellen Beth, author.
Title: Culturally responsive data literacy / Ellen B. Mandinach, WestEd.
Description: Lanham, Maryland : Rowman & Littlefield, [2025] | Includes bibliographical references and index. Identifiers: LCCN 2023059352 (print) | LCCN 2023059353 (ebook) | ISBN 9781538177273 (cloth) | ISBN 9781538177280 (paperback) | ISBN 9781538177297 (epub) Subjects: LCSH: Culturally relevant pedagogy. | Education—Data processing. | Data mining—Moral and ethical aspects.
Classification: LCC LC1099.515.C85 M36 2025 (print) | LCC LC1099.515.C85 (ebook) | DDC 370.117—dc23/eng/20240229
LC record available at https://lccn.loc.gov/2023059352
LC ebook record available at https://lccn.loc.gov/2023059353

To Eli and Houdi, my ever-present muses. Eli always questions my thinking while Houdi quietly purrs advice and encouragement next to my computer. He sometimes even contributes. And to all the dedicated educators who must work in challenging environments with way too little respect: Thank you for all you do. It is such a hard but essential vocation.

Contents

Acknowledgments	vii
Preface	ix
Chapter 1: Introduction: Grounding This Volume From a Personal Perspective	1
Chapter 2: Defining Culturally Responsive Data Literacy	7
Chapter 3: Setting the Landscape for the Scenarios	29
Chapter 4: Introduction to the Scenarios	35
Chapter 5: The Scenarios Continued	71
Chapter 6: Change Is Systemic	109
Chapter 7: What Needs to Happen	117
References	123
Index	129
About the Author	131

Acknowledgments

Many individuals have impacted the work reflected in this volume. I am grateful for their insights, suggestions, and collaborations. First, I would like to acknowledge Susan Mundry of WestEd, who worked with me to think about ways to make data literacy a more relevant, timelier construct. It was her suggestion to add the culturally responsive component to the data literacy for teachers (DLFT) construct. Susan linked me to Saroja Warner, WestEd's then new director of talent development and diversity and now the director of culturally responsive systems. Saroja brought to the work expertise in teacher preparation and diversity. Together, we developed the first forays into what became culturally responsive data literacy (CRDL). Saroja knows teachers, teacher preparation, and cultural responsiveness, contributing to the development of initial resources that could be usable in building educator capacity. Her understanding of an equity mind-set strengthened our work.

The initial work was funded through the Regional Education Laboratory (REL) program, with webinars for REL Northeast and Islands and REL Mid-Atlantic. These webinars allowed us to present the CRDL construct to educator preparation programs as well as local education agencies, attempting to provide awareness to the entire trajectory of educator learning. We later presented the construct in workshops for the Branch Alliance, the Northeast Educational Research Association, and the National Association of State Directors of Teacher Education and Certification. We continue to find venues to bring awareness to CRDL.

I would like to acknowledge Dr. Patricia McHatton of the Branch Alliance and formerly the dean and provost at the University of Texas Rio Grande Valley, who has helped me think about the equity component of CRDL and reach Branch's institutions.

I would especially like to single out Dr. Jori Beck of Old Dominion University and Dr. Jo Beth Jimerson of Texas Christian University for helping me think through the scenarios. Jori reviewed the list of scenario topics and suggested others that are relevant to the topic. She has been a wonderful thought partner. Similarly, Jo and I have worked on data privacy scenarios for administrators from which I have extracted and modified the structure of those scenarios for this volume. Jo understands the needs of educators, and her expertise and experience as a school leader and researcher have strengthened this work. The administrator scenarios, as well as data privacy scenarios for teachers, were developed with funding from and collaboration with the Future of Privacy Forum. I would like to acknowledge the contributions of Jim Siegl and Juliana Cotto from whom I learned a great deal about data privacy. I would also like to acknowledge Diana Nunnaley, with whom I have had many insightful discussions about what is happening with educators in terms of data use and their needs.

The DLFT work was funded first by the Bill and Melinda Gates Foundation, in collaboration with Edith Gummer. It was extended by the Michael & Susan Dell Foundation. The work has transformed significantly from its inception, from trying to understand what it means for an educator to be data literate to the development of DLFT, to an extension of DLFT to data ethics; that is, not only using data effectively but also appropriately.

The work of Dr. Amanda Datnow of the University of California San Diego has been an important impetus for pursuing CRDL. Amanda is a leading voice among data researchers on data for equity. Her work is insightful and impactful. Her work importantly has noted the need to move away from data use for accountability that can have a negative impact on vulnerable students.

I would like to thank the many educators I have met in my career who have impacted my thinking. What you do is so amazing and so very important. You have my respect for persevering under incredibly difficult circumstances. You may be the educators I have met through my research or webinars, or encountered more causally. Discussions with educators such as Joy Schermer of Santa Rosa, California, and Scott Dixon, a retired teacher in Scottsdale, Arizona, have informed my thinking. We have discussed situations they have encountered in the classrooms. Such interactions have stimulated ideas and examples, particularly for the scenarios.

I would like to thank my friends, tennis partners, and colleagues for allowing me to use your pets' names in the scenarios. It is fun to see their names in print and remember our furry friends. And speaking of furry friends, I would like to acknowledge the inspirational trip to Antarctica in January 2023 that provided a jump-start for writing this volume. It was incredibly inspirational to watch the magical ice formations and interact with adorable (and "aromatic") penguins. I began handwriting the scenarios on that trip.

I would also like to acknowledge all my tennis friends and teammates who provided a diversion from my writing and kept me running around and healthy. I single out Sue Holroyd, a tennis pro par excellence. Watching Sue use data to inform how she instructs is a lesson in how to be a masterful teacher but in a different classroom venue. She integrates all sorts of data on the tennis court and then transforms them into actionable, understandable steps to make me a better tennis player—truly data literacy in action. And to Catherine Dunik, Holly Barone, and Kathy Fishman for tennis, pets, support, and friendship.

Thank you to Mark Kerr of Rowman & Littlefield for his interest in this book and its topic; Mark was nothing but positive about the potential impact of this volume. And then to Nathan Davidson for seeing the book to completion after Mark's retirement—thank you for your encouragement and suggestions to make this a better book.

Finally, I thank the two males in my life, Eli and Houdi. Eli often asks me why I cannot write a best seller. He puts up with my passion for tennis, exercise, and writing. He questions my thinking and helps me be more precise. As a data-driven person, he understands data use in many venues but calls me out for some of what he refers to as my PhDuh moments. Houdi is our fur baby. He is my research assistant, sitting by my side while I write or exercise. He even sometimes contributes as he walks across the keyboard, but no coauthorship for him. I love them both, and they make my life so much better.

Preface

Many educators are inadequately prepared to use data effectively, particularly a diverse array of student data to inform their decision making. Educators may have foundational knowledge of assessment literacy but not always data literacy. The lack of educator preparation around data literacy has become a more dire problem as data sources have proliferated and with recognition of the need to respond to the complexities and diversity of students. It is no longer adequate to address students' needs solely based on student performance indicators; thus, the need is pressing to examine a wide range of data that can help educators understand student backgrounds, personal histories, and context—that is, be culturally responsive. Without knowledge of such diverse data sources, educators will continue to view students in a myopic manner that fails to consider the whole child, often sorting the student based on a single metric. Further, many educators, particularly those who serve vulnerable populations, have not been taught how to assume an asset model and take an equity lens to their practice. Educator preparation programs and in-service training have not adequately addressed these needs. Professional organizations, although aware, have not moved to adequately require data literacy or cultural responsiveness through credentialing, licensure, or state standards. These organizations need to take a strong stand and include both constructs in their standards and requirements.

Students are complex. They bring to the classroom unique characteristics that influence how they perform, behave, and function in educational settings. It is incumbent upon educators to recognize the uniqueness of and diversity among students to better meet the needs of all students. To do this, educators must know how to use diverse data sources and demonstrate the skills, knowledge, and dispositions of data literacy. They must also use culturally responsive practice to address the diverse needs of their students. This means understanding students' background, interests, and context while using an asset-based model and an equity mind-set. These are big asks for educators. They require awareness of the importance of data literacy and culturally responsive practices. They require yet another set of skills that often are not addressed in their preservice experiences or subsequently during in-service training.

The objective of this volume is to bring to educators an awareness of culturally responsive data literacy (CRDL). This volume addresses the need to consider all data sources, not just student performance indices. Data are so much more, and educators need to understand the importance of how such diverse data sources can—and should—inform their practice. It is a call to action. This volume explains what CRDL is and how it emerged as an important concept. Perhaps most importantly, this volume provides concrete materials that can be used in preservice and in-service settings to help educators apply CRDL in their practice. It provides an understanding of the roles different stakeholder groups need to play to effect change that will embed CRDL in education. Finally, this volume provides a set of guidelines and concrete recommendations for the implementation of CRDL.

Chapter 1

Introduction: Grounding This Volume From a Personal Perspective

Over the past few years, I have worked with colleagues at WestEd and elsewhere to develop the construct of culturally responsive data literacy. As readers will see in the next chapter, CRDL merges data literacy with culturally responsive practices. Throughout the trajectory of research and development, I began to think about my personal and academic backgrounds that have contributed to this arena of work. In part, the introspection was stimulated by direct or indirect comments about how a white woman could work in cultural responsiveness. Thus, I feel the need to provide a context for this volume. I hope that readers will understand and respect my perspective. This introduction is not intended as a defense but an explanation about why CRDL is important to me and, hopefully, to all educators.

My work for more than two decades has focused on data-driven decision making, particularly data literacy. This is where my expertise lies. My data work has been informed and strengthened by other colleagues working in the data field. My work is better for those collaborations, informed by others' research. Such collegial exchange is fundamental to the scientific process and theory development. Citing other scholars' work with proper attribution is both a learning opportunity (that is, understanding others' work and informing my own) and a statement of the esteem in which I hold their work. Citations of researchers is how the field contextualizes and extends work. I make no pretense about my expertise; it is squarely focused on data-driven decision making, exploring what it means for educators to be data literate. This work produced an initial construct, data literacy for teachers (DLFT; Mandinach & Gummer, 2016a, 2016b, 2016c).

The transformation of DLFT to CRDL was a purposeful response to scholars working in the data arena who identified that data use has been shown to marginalize the most vulnerable students (Datnow, 2017; Datnow & Park, 2018), in part due to the focus on student performance measures that do not adequately reflect what students can do and basically attach a number to the students. Another motivation was accountability that focuses on negativism (Nichols, 2021; Nichols & Berliner, 2007) in contrast to data use for continuous improvement. Data often are seen as threatening, inequitable, and problematic, all tied to accountability. Data use has been accused of fomenting unethical behavior such as gaming the system (Booher-Jennings, 2005) and narrowing the curriculum (Au, 2007). The transformation was also a response to the need to make DLFT more consequential and relevant to the realities of education practice.[1]

The data field has been evolving toward continuous improvement, at least philosophically if not in practice. That is not to say that accountability will disappear. Educators still need test scores to illuminate learning needs, but other and more diverse data sources should and must loom large. There must be a deep, sustainable philosophical and systemic shift to help all students. This is not about sorting students or quantifying them by a single metric. It is about understanding the whole child and incorporating that understanding of children and their contexts to identify strategies to help them succeed.

This volume is also reflective of systems thinking and the need to consider systemic interactions to effect change. Scheetz and Senge (n.d.) have written a seminal article on equity and systemic change. The authors state, "If we are to reconstruct our educational systems to ensure equity for all, systems thinking is an essential skill and the habits of systems thinking must guide our actions" (p. 8). They recognize that everyone has unconscious biases, but school systems work against the needed reflection to consider the consequences and to deal with systemic inequities. They caution against quick fixes that focus on surface factors. They also note that accountability is a pervasive issue that drives the push toward such quick fixes to highly complex problems.

Further, this volume reflects the perspective of allyship.[2] In the pursuit of accuracy, allyship is defined as "the status or role of a person who advocates and actively works for the inclusion of a marginalized or politicized group in all areas of society, not as a member of that group, but in solidarity with its struggle and point of view under its leadership" (Dictionary.com, n.d.). Allyship is relevant in the development of CRDL because it pertains to intersectionality: the interaction between two major bodies of work. As the theory of CRDL has emerged and evolved, the construct has been informed by scholars, researchers, policy makers, and practitioners. No one individual has all the answers, but the differing perspectives have enhanced, clarified, and sometimes corrected my thinking about how data are being used. One need not be an expert in all domains, but it is important to advocate for oneself and for the perspectives and work of others; to describe and promote what relevant stakeholders are doing or need to do to engender progress in theory and practice.

So, given this brief introduction, what gives me the right to discuss CRDL? As I stated, I have worked in the world of data-driven decision making and have observed the good, the bad, and the ugly as educators struggle to become more evidence-based. In 2010, Edith Gummer and I began a quest to operationalize what would become DLFT. We identified more than 50 skills, knowledge, and dispositions (Mandinach & Gummer, 2016a, 2016b, 2016c) in what my husband referred to as the "50 shades of data." Equity and ethics were embedded in the construct but were not sufficiently explicit. DLFT was later informed by the work of Amanda Datnow (2017; Datnow et al., 2021; Datnow & Park, 2018) in her insightful research on equity, including a special journal issue that focused on equity in data use (Braaten et al., 2017; Datnow et al., 2017; Gannon-Slater, 2017; Garner et al., 2017) as well as other scholars (Beck, 2023–2024; Dodman et al., 2021; Lasater et al., 2021). In addition, Bertrand and Marsh (2015, 2021) examined data use in terms of attribution theory and deficit models. These topics are essential to incorporating CRDL into practice. Correspondingly, WestEd adopted both a whole child perspective and an equity focus (Walrond, 2021; Walrond & Romer, 2021). These parallel tracks of work helped to stimulate the transformation to CRDL.

The culturally responsive (Ladson-Billings, 1995, 2006), relevant (Gay, 2018), and sustaining (Paris, 2012; Paris & Alim, 2014) work further informed thinking about how data use could and should assume an equity mind-set. The intention has been for CRDL to take on a whole child perspective: assume an asset model with an equity lens so that educators can gain a more comprehensive understanding of each student. Saroja Warner was a collaborator in the initial exploration of CRDL. That work is the foundation for this volume (Mandinach & Warner, 2021, 2022; Mandinach et al., 2019, 2020; Mandinach et al., 2020; Warner, 2021). The CRDL work has also been informed by Patricia McHatton, vice president of the Branch Alliance, an organization that focuses on diversification of the educator work pool, and a former dean of two schools of education.

Research and practice often conflict. Research recommends certain practices, but the real world of education works against those recommendations because of the systemic complexities. Take, for example, a comment from the director of special education at one of the largest districts in the country. The individual said there was no way that they could individualize to the needs of all their special education students: there simply are too many. The irony here is that special education, in contrast to general education, has had a much longer history of using data to address individual students' needs (Hamilton et al., 2009).

Individualization or adaptive learning (Corno, 2008) requires adept educators. It requires an understanding of individual differences (Cronbach & Snow, 1977). It also relies on the forms of knowledge educators must have (Shulman, 1986, 1987). In fact, Shulman's seven forms of teacher knowledge became part of the DLFT construct. But DLFT was not sufficiently explicit to capture the needed nuances of an equity mind-set, so colleagues at WestEd and I began to examine the works of Ladson-Billings, Gay, and others. Taking a systems approach, we began to explore how to introduce the concept of CRDL into educator preparation programs (Mandinach et al., 2019, 2020) and local education agencies (Mandinach et al., 2020).

Another example is telling. I have been pushing the data field to think broadly about what data are, not just consider data to be quantifiable and test scores. An interaction with an educator in Vermont is relevant. Asked what data are, the individual said, "I am now the superintendent, so data are test scores. But when I was a teacher, data were so much more." I typically ask audiences what data are to gain an understanding of their perspectives and how broadly they think about data. Most of the responses focus on test scores or more generally, different forms of student performance indices. People most often do not think beyond student learning. Cultural shifts are working against the broad definition beyond student performance in states such as Florida where politics mandate that educators ignore such important constructs as grit and socio-emotional well-being.

Let us consider the issue of bias, which will be explored more deeply in this volume. In education and elsewhere, people make assumptions about others, sometimes with terrible consequences. Here I choose to think broadly about diversity and inclusion, beyond race and ethnicity, to many other background characteristics. It could be a special status such as native language or disability. It could be geographical issues such as coming from a rural school that does not have a full range of course offerings. It could be a designation of homelessness, emancipated minor, military child, or foster care. There are many possibilities. Bias could impact perceptions of and interactions with students with such designations. I use a few personal examples to help readers understand incidents that impacted my thinking about CRDL well before I became an educational psychologist.

I grew up in New Hampshire in a small, rural school district. I was the only Jewish student. When the major holidays occurred, the school determined that my absences for religious reasons were unexcused. The school failed me for those days because they had never encountered anyone else who was Jewish. Some serious discussion by my parents with school leadership helped the educators to understand that Yom Kippur was no different from scheduling Good Friday as a holiday. In retrospect, it is hard to determine whether this situation was unconscious bias or simply unaware educators. It was a long time ago when small New England towns had little diversity.

I recall a colleague having a similar issue as an educator in rural New Jersey. She argued with the district that Christmas and Good Friday were not her holidays, and she offered to work those days instead of Yom Kippur and Rosh Hashanah. The argument did not work. As another example, some years ago a school in the Chicago Public Schools scheduled its annual pictures during a religious holiday. A segment of the student population and faculty were negatively impacted by the scheduling issue. Similarly, scheduling an important event on Ramadan would impact Muslim students. With increasing diversity, holiday celebrations have become even more difficult. Take, for example, a large school district in California that has many Pacific Rim groups, each with their own New Year. How should such celebrations be handled to attain cultural sensitivity? How do you schedule school events and sports around holidays for all religions without showing bias or insensitivity? And some students' religion prevents them from participating in any celebratory event.

As our students become increasingly diverse, it is incumbent upon educators to be responsive to the many forms of difference and student backgrounds. Here is another example from a speech by then second lady Dr. Jill Biden (2016) at the American Educational Research Association annual meeting. Dr. Biden focused on the special needs of students from military families. It is unclear how many educators are aware of the circumstances and needs that these children encounter. Some of my colleagues and friends who teach at educator preparation programs where there are major military installations have told me that they have no special classes to help bring awareness to future and current educators about military students. These students often move from school to school without an opportunity to make lasting social connections and are likely to have disjointed educational histories. They also may have anxieties around the parent or family member who is deployed and in harm's way, or worse, they may come from a Gold Star family. Knowledge of such characteristics is essential as data sources to help educators better serve these students. This is an issue of awareness and preparedness, not necessarily bias. Dr. Biden's speech was incredibly impactful, and it brought attention to the audience about a category of students about which most people likely are not aware.

Actions have consequences, and conscious or unconscious bias can be involved. Take, for example, a teacher who does not feel comfortable expressing an opinion for fear of reprisal because the sentiment is in some way controversial or unpopular. One can easily imagine this happening now, given the divisive political environment. A teacher makes a comment in class. A student goes home and reports it to her parents. The parents complain to the school, and the teacher is censured or even fired. In Arizona where I live, one candidate for governor in 2022 proposed installing cameras in every classroom; the purpose was to ensure that teachers say nothing untoward to offend any student. My immediate reaction was that this would be incredibly intrusive and moreover, a violation of student privacy regulations. I asked a friend who is a department chair in a California high school for her opinion. It surprised me. The teacher reported that she would be fine with the cameras to protect herself: firm evidence would support her practice if a student complained about something she said or did. That said, educators in Arizona reacted to the camera proposal was indignation and fear.

In another example, a smart student raises her hand and almost always answers questions correctly. Fellow students begin to harass her to the point that she is negatively conditioned to no longer volunteer answers. Such harassment or bullying can easily have a lifelong impact on a student. The lesson here is that the educational process is complex and has many potential land mines that can permanently damage educators' interactions with students or other educators and interactions among students. People can be intentionally cruel. People can be blind to what may harm others. Awareness, sensitivity, and responsiveness are very much needed.

Actions do have ethical consequences. More recently in Arizona, the superintendent of instruction at the Arizona Department of Education instituted a call-in hotline for parents to report "inappropriate lessons" (Kunichoff, 2023a, 2023b). The hotline was flooded with calls, many of them pranks. In response to the intended objective of the hotline, a columnist in the

Arizona Republic suggested that parents call in, not to report "inappropriate lessons" but to laud good educators (Montini, 2023). How would or should a district administrator act in response to one of the reports? Is such a data source valid and accurate? Is the reporting retribution or politically motivated? What consequences should there be from a false report? These questions undergird the ethical use of data and evidence.

The point of these real accounts is to illustrate that bias, equity, and ethics come in many forms. To be clear, in no way do I want to be disingenuous or offend anyone with the content of this volume. CRDL and the underlying concepts can push the envelope. This may be especially true in the highly politicized environment that the education sector has become. Teachers fear for their jobs because they are afraid of saying something, even an innocent statement, that may offend a student or parent. Books are being banned by a single parent or stakeholder who is offended by something, even if they did not read the books (Mueller, 2023; Sangalang & Wagner, 2023), and most recently dictionaries and encyclopedias are at risk in Florida (Cohen, 2024). Many of the books go to the heart of diversity and equity. Even showing classic works of art such as Michelangelo's statue of David has been found offensive and been banned in places. One could ask what are the legitimate boundaries of bias and offensive material? Apparently, topics in these books and reference materials make people uncomfortable.

In contrast, the guiding questions on unconscious bias prepared for and first disseminated by the Regional Educational Laboratory Northeast (Mandinach et al., 2019) are meant to make people uncomfortable to help them confront such perceptions and stimulate deep thought about the consequences of actions. These questions appear in chapter 2. The objective is to help educators think broadly and inclusively about the whole child. Every child brings his uniqueness to school and to life. As educators, we must capitalize on the uniqueness, students' backgrounds, and their life histories and circumstances. This is why the components of CRDL stress the need to expand the idea of diverse data sources. It is why the data literacy component of CRDL is so important and an essential companion to cultural responsiveness. I make no pretense to be an expert on the "CR" of CRDL. It is why my collaborations with Warner have been informative.

For CRDL to be meaningful, we need to rethink and redefine what we mean by data. We need to broaden the definition of educationally relevant data. We must take seriously the need to address the whole child. We must think beyond test scores, student performance indices, and accountability data. This is a fundamental paradigm shift around data use. It is the challenge that is foundational to this volume.

OVERVIEW OF THE VOLUME

This volume will walk the reader through the research and theories that underlie CRDL, leading to the presentation of authentic scenarios that can be used to help educators acquire CRDL, followed by how to effect change, and finally actionable recommendations to embed CRDL into education.

Chapter 2 provides the reader with an overview first of DLFT, then cultural responsiveness. The chapter explores the foundational research that led to the definition of DLFT and the identification of the skills, knowledge, and dispositions required of educators to be considered data literate. It highlights the data literacy skills that are particularly relevant in CRDL. It describes relevant equity-oriented data research and how it has impacted thinking about CRDL. The chapter also links relevant concepts such as accountability pressures, attribution theory, deficit and asset models, the whole child approach, and confirmation bias. The chapter explains the need to merge the two topics into CRDL and provides a working definition. The chapter then discusses the three main perspectives on cultural responsiveness: cultural responsiveness, cultural relevance, and culturally sustaining practices. The chapter concludes with the guiding questions from the Regional Educational Laboratory presentations (Mandinach et al., 2019).

Chapter 3 examines the landscape into which CRDL must be embedded. The chapter identifies state standards and codes of ethics as they pertain to data literacy and cultural responsiveness. It is important to understand how these concepts are addressed in the standards, reflecting what states deem to be important skills that educators must possess.

Chapter 4 introduces the scenarios through a user's guide and primer. The chapter explains the structure of the scenarios, how they are meant to reflect authentic situations that educators might experience, and how CRDL could be used to address the situations portrayed in the scenarios. The chapter presents the first half of the scenarios; the second half is presented in chapter 5.

Chapter 6 explores the complex interactions among institutions and agencies in the quest to embed CRDL in educational practice. The chapter identifies seven stakeholder groups within the complex system: the U.S. Department of Education; state education agencies; local education agencies; professional organizations; professional development and technical assistance providers; and testing organizations. A systems mapping is depicted, and the roles of each stakeholder group are described with the identification of the interactions with other stakeholder groups.

Chapter 7 provides the actionable steps needed to ensure that CRDL becomes part of educational practice. The chapter lays out recommended steps but notes many of the challenges to effecting change. The recommended steps are intended to provide a roadmap to implementation. To conclude the volume on a positive note, the chapter will explicitly describe a vision for how CRDL can positively impact educational practice.

NOTES

1. I would like to acknowledge the collaboration with Susan Mundry, the colleague who suggested broadening DLFT to CRDL. Without her suggestion, the construct likely would have remained in its original form.

2. Thank you to Mark Kerr for describing the role of allyship in educational practice.

Chapter 2

Defining Culturally Responsive Data Literacy

This chapter walks through the creation of CRDL, grounded in the development of DLFT and culturally responsive practice. The chapter begins with the research base that laid out the DLFT construct. It describes the DLFT skills, knowledge, and dispositions and how they translate to CRDL. The chapter then examines the data literature that focuses on equity, including accountability, asset versus deficit models, attribution theory, and confirmation bias. It explores the various perspectives on culturally responsive practices. Finally, the chapter discusses the merger and the creation of CRDL.

Let me ground this review in a piece of evidence that indicates that appropriate data use is gaining traction in education and beyond. The day after the 2021 presidential inauguration, an executive order was released indicating the importance of data to inform equity and then followed by a report showing subsequent progress (White House, 2021, 2023). The executive order said that a "first step to promoting equity in government action is to gather the data necessary to inform that effort" (p. 1). An outgrowth of that order was the creation of the Equitable Data Working Group (2022) that released a set of recommendations and a vision, followed by a progress report (2023). According to the working group (2022), "equitable data illuminate opportunities for targeted actions that will result in demonstrably improved outcomes for underserved communities" (p. 3). The sheer fact that a working group at the highest level of the federal government exists to address equitable data use is an explicit message about its emerging importance. This working group deals with data well beyond education, but the premises most certainly can be applied to education.

DATA LITERACY FOR TEACHERS

The DLFT construct is based on years of research and theory development and has been informed by many experts in the fields of data use, professional development, and practice. The work began in 2010. The following year, more than 50 experts came together to explore and help define data literacy. At that time, there was no concrete definition, something that the field sorely needed to be able to communicate to educators, policy makers, professional organizations, and others which skills are involved in using data in educational practice. Such a definition would enable data literacy to be embedded in professional standards, educator preparation, and professional development because if you cannot explain what a construct is, it is hard to discuss, teach, and implement.

We examined every professional development program. We reviewed every resource and book available at that time to survey the landscape. We invited providers and resource developers to collaborate. Among those resources were "how-to" books and guides, some based on research (e.g., Boudett et al., 2005; Love et al., 2008) and others less so (Bambrick-Santoyo, 2010; Bernhardt, 2004). The culmination of the analyses and convening was a report that identified more than 100 skills (Mandinach & Gummer, 2011). Further refinement was conducted over the next few years and ultimately some 50 skills, knowledges, and dispositions were determined to be the most salient (Mandinach & Gummer, 2016b, 2016c).

Because assessment literacy and data literacy often are confused, this convening examined the differences between them. There has been a frustrating conflation, due in part to the fact that assessment data are perhaps the most pervasive data that teachers use. The result of the discussion was a clear delineation whereby assessment literacy was seen as a component of data literacy because assessment data are only one form of data. Data literacy was seen as a much broader construct, covering many diverse forms of data, including student test scores and assessment data. Sadly, the conflation continues and plays a key role in the push toward CRDL rather than DLFT.

DEFINITION AND STRUCTURE

Before we began our research and theory development, most discussion in the data field was about data-driven decision making, for which there are numerous definitions (e.g., Hamilton et al., 2009). Little attention focused solely on data literacy. Thus, our attempt to define the construct was timely and hopefully impactful. DLFT is defined by Mandinach and Gummer (2016b) as

> the ability to transform information into actionable instructional knowledge and practices by collecting, analyzing, and interpreting all types of data (assessment, school climate, behavioral, snapshot, longitudinal, moment-to-moment, etc.) to help determine instructional steps. It combines an understanding of data with standards, disciplinary knowledge and practices, curricular knowledge, pedagogical content knowledge, and an understanding of how children learn. (p. 14)

This definition is much more comprehensive than preexisting and cursory definitions. In parallel, I worked with the Data Quality Campaign (2014) to develop a simple way of communicating data literacy to policy makers and others with a focus on all educators. That definition, intended as a sound byte, is:

> Data-literate educators continuously, effectively, and ethically access, interpret, act on, and communicate multiple types of data from state, local, classroom, and other sources to improve professional roles and responsibilities. (p. 1)

The two definitions have similarities. At that time, the Data Quality Campaign was prophetic in foreseeing the pressing need for ethical data use, not just effective data use. Their definition does not recognize the kinds of knowledge and skills educators need or the kinds of data because the focus of and objective for the definition was not the same as for DLFT. Part of the objective for DLFT was to stimulate discussions and further research while impacting and informing professional organizations and practice.

DLFT is informed by Shulman's (1986, 1987) seven forms of knowledge that teachers must have. They include content knowledge; curriculum knowledge; knowledge of learners and their characteristics; knowledge of educational ends, purposes, and values; general pedagogical knowledge; pedagogical content knowledge; and knowledge of educational contexts. These are foundational forms of knowledge that impact how data are used. At the most fundamental level, teachers need content knowledge and pedagogical content knowledge that can lead to instructional action. Data use becomes the third component from which knowledge of data should inform both content and pedagogical knowledge so that teachers can make decisions. In fact, an earlier version of our data literacy framework focused only on the triangulation of content knowledge, pedagogical content knowledge, and data use (Gummer & Mandinach, 2015).

DLFT takes the form of an iterative inquiry cycle in which there are five components:

- The first component is identifying a problem of practice and framing questions.
- The second component is called use data. It comprises more than two dozen skills that are the basis of data use. Frankly, we could not think of a better and more descriptive title for this component.
- The third component is transforming data into information. This component is based on a fundamental concept of data use in which data are transformed into information and ultimately to actionable knowledge. Data differ from information because data are in the raw form whereas information is based on data that have been manipulated in some way.
- The fourth component is transforming information into a decision. This is the pedagogical aspect of the process.
- The final component is evaluating outcomes.

These five components form a cyclical loop rather than a linear continuum. Just because a decision has been made and results evaluated does not mean that the process is complete. There is always more work to be done.

COMPONENTS, KNOWLEDGE, SKILLS, AND DISPOSITIONS

The more than 50 knowledge, skills, and dispositions are aligned across the five components of DLFT that form the iterative inquiry cycle. I lay out each and link them to CRDL in terms of their centrality to the newer construct, with CRDL introduced later in this chapter. It is important to understand the scope of the DLFT skills first, then extrapolate to CRDL. Also, to be clear, there are instances when I indicate that a skill is not central to CRDL. By this I mean that the specific skill is more a part of data literacy and less about the culturally responsive part of CRDL.

IDENTIFY A PROBLEM OF PRACTICE AND FRAME QUESTIONS

Let me preface this component with a general comment. The field often refers to a problem of practice. The framing is negative. It speaks to a deficit model. In retrospect, I now prefer a title such as Identify a Pressing Educational Issue and Frame Questions, which assumes an asset model. The renaming is more than semantic. It is essential to rethink to terminology we use to support an asset-based perspective.

Articulate a problem of practice. This is framed in a negative tone. The objective is for educators to understand that there is an issue or a question to which data can be applied to inform decision making. If termed positively, this is important to CRDL.

Understand the context at a student level. The objective is for educators to understand what the situation is around the specific student that will then enable the collection of targeted data to address that situation, for that child. This is critical to CRDL.

Understand the context at the school level. The skill pertains to educators' understanding the broader context of the school. It might be particularly relevant if educators observe a particular group of students, rather than an individual student, struggling or being underserved. Perhaps something within the school context is causing that to happen. This also can be important to CRDL.

Involve other participants or stakeholders. Students do not live in isolation. Using data may involve other educators, the students themselves, their parents or guardians, or other relevant stakeholders. This skill speaks to the need to address the whole child and is therefore key to CRDL.

Understand student privacy. Protecting student data is important, especially if the data are of a sensitive nature, such as behavioral data, medical data, and personally identifiable information. Knowledge of data privacy is key to CRDL and fundamentally is about data ethics—that is, using data appropriately.

USE DATA

This domain is an amalgam of different skills that relate to data use. There is no sufficiently descriptive title for the domain as it contains 27 skills and forms of knowledge. These skills are fundamental to being able to use data effectively. Further, these skills are essential to DLFT, but some may be less central to the transformation to CRDL.

Identify possible sources of data. Using multiple and diverse sources of data is an essential skill for CRDL. Educators need different forms of data to triangulate across multiple measures.

Understand the purpose of different data sources. Educators must understand the importance of using and triangulating among different data sources to inform their decisions and the purposes or rationales for each of the sources. This is perhaps the most important skill for CRDL as it moves the focus away from just quantifiable test scores.

Understand how to generate data. Classrooms are generating data all the time, whether hard, quantitative data or softer, observational data. Some data may be moment to moment, whereas others may be long-term. Educators must recognize the differences, when to use such data, and how to interpret them. This is important to CRDL.

Understand assessment. It is central to understanding student learning. Educators must understand different kinds of assessments and the purposes for which they should be used. This is more about assessment literacy than CRDL.

Use formative and summative assessments. This is fundamental to assessment literacy and relevant to CRDL, given the recognition that high-stakes assessments have been shown to marginalize groups of students and that formative assessments are closer to local instruction.

Develop sound assessment design and implementation. This is fundamental to assessment literacy—that is, how to design an assessment that links appropriately to the curricula and that can generate the kinds of results that will be informative. This is not central to CRDL unless the assessment is found to be biased toward groups of students.

Understand data properties. Educators must understand different kinds and levels of data and how they are appropriate in given situations. This includes composites, strand level, item level, and total scores. It is not the most central to CRDL.

Use multiple measures/sources of data. This skill is foundational to assessment literacy and data literacy. Educators must understand the importance of using multiple measures as a way of increasing reliability. It is essential to CRDL.

Use qualitative and quantitative data. Many data important to CRDL may be qualitative rather than quantitative. Educators must understand both forms of data and that not all data are numbers and quantifiable.

Understand the specificity of data to the question/problem. This skill entails knowing how to align data to the identified problem, question, or issue. This is important to CRDL but needs to be framed in a positive manner.

Understand which data are appropriate. This skill pertains to recognizing which data are relevant to a particular question or issue. It goes to the heart of validity and is important to CRDL.

Understand data quality. Data quality is essential to making sound decisions. Educators must understand the implications of using data that lack in quality. This is central to CRDL.

Understand elements of data accuracy, appropriateness, and completeness. These are components of data quality. Data must also be relevant, reliable, and valid. Educators must understand the implications of using data that are inaccurate, inappropriate for a particular question, or incomplete and the kinds of inferences and conclusions that potentially can harm students. This is essential to CRDL.

Understand how to access data. Data must be readily accessible for educators, whether in files or in data systems in electronic format. This is not central to CRDL.

Find, locate, access, and retrieve data. Educators must know where data are and how to access them. This is not central to CRDL.

Use technologies to support data use. There has been a proliferation of technologies to support data use, including large-scale data warehouses, data dashboards, early warning systems, and apps on mobile devices. This is fundamental to data use now with educators being faced with so much data from so many sources. It may not be central to CRDL.

Understand how to analyze data. Analysis brings meaning to the data, often through statistical procedures for quantitative data. It is fundamental to data use but less so to CRDL.

Understand statistics and psychometrics. Educators need to have a fundamental understanding of elementary statistics and measurement concepts, such as reliability and validity. It is not central to CRDL.

Manage data. This skill involves knowing how to code, store, and arrange data in a systematic manner. It is not central to CRDL.

Organize data. This skill entails making manageable or meaningful representations of data. It is not necessarily most central to CRDL.

Prioritize data. This involves determining which data are the most important for a given situation or decision. CRDL becomes important here if educators insert unconscious bias or preconceived notions.

Examine data. This skill involves scrutinizing data to make meaning. It is fundamental to data use but not necessarily CRDL.

Integrate data. Integration involves pulling together data in a meaningful way. It is fundamental to data use but not necessarily CRDL.

Manipulate data. Handling data is part of fundamental data use but not as important to CRDL.

Drill down into data. It is important to understand which level of data will be the most informative for a given situation. Often the most informative is at the item level, which can be linked directly to a student's understanding of a concept. Higher levels of data may be less informative for modifying instruction. This is important to individualize instruction and for CRDL.

Aggregate data. Aggregating data is about the whole group. There are times when such a view of data is important. Depending on the intent, this could be part of CRDL.

Disaggregate data. It is important for educators to examine subgroup performance by breaking down the data. This is important to CRDL if it is done without blaming certain subgroups for their performance.

TRANSFORM DATA INTO INFORMATION

Data and information are different. Data are typically in raw form whereas information has been manipulated in some way—for example, summarized or synthesized so that the user can ultimately act. This component contains nine skills that help to transform data into information.

Consider the impact and consequences. Impact is important. Consequences can be intended or unintended based on a decision. Users must consider what might happen based on the information. It will inform which decisions can or should be made. This skill is essential to CRDL, because decision makers sometimes fail to consider what might be the potential harms or unintended consequences of specific actions.

Generate hypothetical connections to instruction. This skill involves foreseeing or predicting what might happen if certain action steps are taken. The ability to consider possible outcomes can mitigate potential problems that might happen from different courses of action. This is critical for CRDL.

Test assumptions. It is important to consider which assumptions are being made based on the information at hand. The information might be incomplete or inadequate. There might be indications that something is amiss. This skill is different from making assumptions about students, something that could lead to confirmation bias. It is about considering or vetting one's thinking. This skill is critical to CRDL.

Understand how to interpret data. The interpretation process gives meaning to the data. Educators make meaning based on the data and information. The process must not be impacted by unconscious or confirmation bias. Thus, this is an essential part of CRDL.

Understand and use data displays and representations. Data often are displayed in graphical representations such as tables, graphs, and charts. Educators must know how to use such displays. This is not a critical part of CRDL.

Assess patterns and trends. Graphical displays often will show trends in data. Teachers can discern trends for individual students, groups, or the class through such displays. It can help them understand how a student or groups of students are doing along a trajectory of learning. This skill is important to CRDL to map individual learning as well as to highlight group or class trends.

Probe for causality. This skill involves trying to understand why certain things have happened. Educators often speak of root causes. Trying to understand the basis for an event, performance, or something else is important to CRDL.

Use statistics. Educators do not need to be statisticians, but they do need to understand and use fundamental statistics. It is not central to CRDL.

Synthesize diverse data. A foundational part of measurement is using diverse and multiple measures from which to make decisions. Particularly for CRDL, triangulating diverse data sources can help educators to better understand the whole child. This is one of the most important CRDL skills.

Articulate inferences and conclusions. Educators need to be able to describe the conclusions they have drawn from the inquiry cycle. Articulating the inferences can help educators check their own thinking. This is important to CRDL.

Summarize and explain data. This skill involves pulling together the various sources of data and making meaning from those data. This is part of CRDL.

TRANSFORM INFORMATION INTO A DECISION

This component is the pedagogical part of the decision-making cycle. Originally, it was referred to as pedagogical decision making. The focus here is on how the data and information are transformed into actionable instructional or other forms of decisions.

Determine next instructional steps. This skill is the heart of pedagogy. The educators must take the information and determine, based on the evidence, the most effective instructional (or whatever the decision topic is) steps. This is part of CRDL.

Monitor student performance. As teachers act, they must observe what is happening with their students to determine what differences are being made. This is also part of CRDL.

Diagnose what students need. Teachers need to understand their students and base their instructional decisions on both the strengths and the weaknesses. CRDL comes into play here with the focus on student strengths, rather than just remediating their weaknesses.

Make instructional adjustments. This pertains to the knowledge of what instructional options are available and which are appropriate, given that the context is important. This is central to pedagogical knowledge and pedagogical content knowledge. Making adjustments that are responsive to student needs is very much a part of CRDL.

Understand the context for the decision. This skill means that teachers must understand the needs of their students and make determinations about action steps based on that information. This is part of CRDL.

EVALUATE THE OUTCOME

The fifth component examines the outcome of the decision, which then allows for the iterative cycle of data use to continue.

Reexamine the original question or problem. Again, this skill needs to be revised to reflect a positive or asset approach. Because data use is cyclical, even though a decision may have been made and the results evaluated, you never are really done. There is always more to do. Therefore, it is important to determine the extent to which the question has been adequately addressed or what other actions might need to be taken. Adding the asset approach then makes this more relevant to CRDL.

Compare performance pre- and post-decision. This helps to determine whether the action steps had a positive or the intended impact. This skill is not as central to CRDL as others.

Monitor changes in classroom practice. Evaluating the impact of a decision requires a level of introspection about the resulting changes. This skill relates to the attribution work of Bertrand and Marsh (2015) in which results could be attributed to instruction, nonmalleable student characteristics, the nature of an assessment, and student understanding.

Attributions to students for failure is deficit thinking. Attributions to what might be responsively changed instructionally allows teachers to take positive steps based on the results. This is key to CRDL.

Monitor student changes in performance. This is similar to the prior skill. It is critical to examine whether decisions have positively or negatively impacted students and determine what modifications need to be made. This also is critical to CRDL.

Consider the need for iterative decision cycles. Fundamental to data-driven decision making is its cyclical nature. Just because data have been collected, analyzed, and acted upon does not mean the process ends. The decision and the subsequent actionable steps then feed into further data collection and actions. This is part of CRDL.

DISPOSITIONS

Dispositions do not easily fit into the skills and knowledge of the five components. Instead, they are seen as generic habits of mind that are part of teaching.

Belief that all students can learn. This disposition goes to the heart of equity. If teachers do not believe that a particular student can learn, they will behave accordingly through conscious forms of bias. Therefore, this disposition is essential to CRDL.

Belief in data/think critically. Believing in the use of data and realizing its potential will help to motivate effective, appropriate data use. Therefore, this belief is important to CRDL.

Belief that continuous improvement in education requires a continuous inquiry cycle. This disposition is part of the philosophical shift from data for accountability to data for continuous improvement. It speaks to the foundational purpose for data use—that is, helping all children learn and improve. Educators must believe that the use of data can inform their practice and that the cycle of data use is continuous, not finite. This is essential to CRDL.

Ethical use of data, including the protection of privacy and confidentiality of data. Many would equate the ethical and appropriate use of data with an equity mind-set. For sure, that linkage is essential. Ethical data use should and must be central to any form of data use for whatever purpose. Appropriate, responsible data use must be a foundational disposition for all educators and is a central part of CRDL.

Collaboration. Data use often occurs in data teams, content teams, grade-level teams, or other forms of interaction among educators. Discussing data responsibly to find solutions and strategies should be a mind-set for all educators. It is important to CRDL.

Communication with multiple audiences. Not only do educators communicate with and about data among themselves, but they must also communicate with their students, parents, the community, and other stakeholders. They must know how to reflect data accurately in their communications and ensure that the communications are objective, accurate, and unbiased, all key to CRDL.

DATA RESEARCH THAT IS RELEVANT TO EQUITY

Research on data use has addressed equity in a variety of ways. Some research targets equity as a topic, whereas other research addresses topics that relate to equity and cultural responsiveness and have been crucial in the broadening of the DLFT construct. Topics of relevance here include equity, accountability, asset and deficit models, attributions, and confirmation bias.

Equity

Equity must be an explicit emphasis in educational data use (Park, 2018). According to Datnow and colleagues (2017), equity is about fairness and disparities. To attain an equity focus, educators must have the capacity to use data and understand the importance of using diverse data sources (Diamond & Cooper, 2016; Mandinach & Gummer, 2016b). Data must address teaching and learning with an equity lens (Gannon-Slater et al., 2017). Educators must invoke an asset orientation that focuses on students' strengths while avoiding deficit thinking (Bertrand & Marsh, 2021). An equity model also requires organizational and leadership support. Leadership around data use has been one of the most acknowledged findings in the data literature (Hamilton et al., 2009). Leaders provide the vision for data use, but that vision must be decoupled from accountability (Datnow & Hubbard, 2015). Leaders provide the needed support for data use through data teams and coaches, dedicated work time, and creating a data culture that is grounded in trust rather than an environment that promotes shaming and blaming.

Data use with an equity focus should not be cursory or superficial (Hoover & Abrams, 2013); in-depth analyses are needed to address fundamental root cause questions. Superficiality can lead to educators who fail to engage in in-depth examinations of student performances and cultural differences. A major driver here is accountability. Accountability policies often ignore cultural differences and fail to promote deeper examination of informative data (Garner et al., 2017). The superficiality reinforces inequities and leads to marginalization. Garner and colleagues also note that such policies promote a mind-set toward remediation rather than addressing systemic causes, similar to the quick fixes that Scheetz and Senge (n.d.) note.

Dodman and colleagues (2021) frame equity-oriented data use as critical data-driven decision making that reveals opportunity gaps through structures and practices. The authors claim that data-driven decision making inherently promotes systemic inequities through implicit bias and structural oppression. In contrast, critical data-driven decision making emphasizes that educators must recognize the underlying assumptions of data use in terms of equity. A major part of this approach is to question accountability. The authors present a framework and espouse the idea of equity literacy that raises awareness of inequity and oppression while stressing the need for meaningful and diverse data that address students' needs.

Implicit bias is related to fallacies in cognitive processing and ladders of influence in decision making (Argyris & Schon, 1974). Generally, fallacies occur when decisions are made based on beliefs rather than data, facts, and evidence. These fallacies may be conscious or unconscious, intended or unintended. These biases skew the data being collected, the analytic processes, the interpretations drawn, and the actions taken.

Accountability

As has been noted, accountability pressures educators in many ways (Au, 2007; Beck, 2023–2024; Berliner, 2011; Hargreaves & Braun, 2013; Nichols, 2021; Nichols & Berliner, 2007). The accountability issue and equity seem to be polarized components. Accountability is seen as a sorting mechanism. As Datnow (2017) notes, accountability has been shown to marginalize vulnerable students. Accountability measures provide granularity for some forms of decisions but not others, particularly at the instructional level. Accountability sometimes forces educators to do unethical things in the name of succeeding. They can game the system. Educators can focus only on a subset of students (Booher-Jennings, 1995; Diamond & Spillane, 2004), ignoring students at either end of the performance continuum. Accountability can narrow the curriculum to teach only to the test (Au, 2007). Accountability pressure can cause good educators to do things that are not so good in their quest to make their schools look good (Mandinach & Jimerson, 2021).

Large-scale educational policies and programs such as No Child Left Behind and Race to the Top marginalize vulnerable student groups because they fail to address the root causes of student performance (Garner et al., 2017). Students cannot and should not be summarized by a single number or test score. This oversimplifies complex constructs. It promotes remediation rather than instructional improvement. Accountability leads to inequities (Diamond & Cooper, 2007). As Garner and colleagues (2017) note, test data do not generate "meaningful consideration of diversity and equity" (p. 421). For data use to have an equity focus without threat or evaluation, educators must look beyond test scores (Beck, 2023–2024; Lasater et al., 2021).

In addition, professional development around data use typically does not focus on data for instructional improvement but, rather, on the use of the accountability measures (Datnow & Hubbard, 2015). Such a focus takes a short-term perspective with an emphasis on compliance, improving test scores, and quick fixes. Further, many educators distrust such data in terms of instructional improvement. Such data use is conflated with accountability where educators rarely go beyond quantitative measures (e.g., test scores) (Mandinach & Gummer, 2016b). Thus, even professional development providers in the field of data may not be addressing the full scope of data sources and promoting an equity mind-set.

Asset and Deficit Models

A key precept of culturally responsive practice is to use an asset model rather than a deficit model throughout educational practice when making interpretations, drawing conclusions, taking actions, and communicating. A deficit model focuses on the deficiencies of students. It is framed in a negative manner, such as remediating a learning deficit or addressing a problem of practice. It reinforces bias (Bertrand & Marsh, 2021). Deficit models blame students for failure. Deficit thinking perpetuates a focus on accountability measures with a goal to view students as numbers, not as people (Lasater et al., 2021). It also perpetuates inequities. It focuses on students' weaknesses that must be corrected.

In contrast, an asset model focuses on students' strengths, interests, and backgrounds. It takes a positive approach to students as individuals, not just numbers to be sorted. Lasater and colleagues (2021) suggest four strategies to establish a nonevaluative, asset-based culture among educators:

1. establish trust among colleagues through effective collaboration,
2. provide support to the educators,
3. make decisions with data that are most relevant to the decision, and
4. create an environment with shared ownership.

Attributions

Attribution theory is relevant to the interpretations drawn from and consequences of data use. Attributions are how people explain or perceive actions. They can be internal or external. They can be stable or unstable. They also differ in terms of controllability. Attributions are central to making sense and shape the expectations educators have of their students. They influence the kinds of interpretations educators may make and the actions they may take in their instructional practice. Bertrand and Marsh (2015) examined the types of attributions teachers made in response to student performance. The authors developed four models of attribution:

1. instruction,
2. student understanding,
3. the nature of the test, and
4. student characteristics.

Attributions to student characteristics are especially relevant to CRDL. If educators attribute poor student performance to nonmalleable student characteristics that are uncontrollable, stable, and external factors, such interpretations can lead to deficit thinking and shaming and blaming. The thinking would be: A student who is X cannot do Y, and I can't do much about it because the factors cannot be controlled. In contrast, teachers may look to their instruction or the assessment method, both of which can be modified. Teachers can adjust their instruction to student needs. They can find more sensitive assessment methods. Attributions say a great deal about what educators are thinking, their beliefs, and what actions they may take from examining data.

Confirmation Bias

Confirmation bias is related to attributions. This bias occurs when people confirm outcomes based on preexisting beliefs. They interpret the outcomes to support their own perspectives (Nickerson, 1998). Confirmation bias can be found in educational practice in several ways that cause educators to examine data about a certain student or group of students in a way that confirms their beliefs, regardless of the results. Take, for example, the stereotype that all Asian students are good at mathematics. Teachers will see the results from that perspective, and the bias will shape their expectations of these students. It is a bias that characterizes students because of educators' beliefs and expectations. Confirmation bias, like attributions, can explain away failure or poor performance. For example, the football coach designs what he thinks is a play that will win the game. He targets his star receiver, assuming that he rarely drops the ball. The interpretations would be very different if the quarterback connects with the receiver for a touchdown than if the receiver drops the ball or the ball is not thrown properly. According to Datnow and Hubbard (2015), educators often use data to affirm their beliefs through unconscious sensemaking.

Culturally Responsive Practice and Teaching

I open this section with a brief discussion of diversity, equity, and inclusion that are foundational to cultural responsiveness. Venkateswaran and colleagues (2023) provided succinct definitions of the three concepts and outlined how each is manifested by researchers. I draw from this work and apply the paradigm to educators.

- They define *diversity* as "acknowledging psychological, physical, and social differences as well as differences as a result of systemic cumulative advantages or systemic cumulative barriers to opportunities" (p. 3). According to the authors, the manifestation would be for educators to acknowledge and consider biases they may hold and the assumptions that may impact their practice. Educators must confront and introspect about their conscious biases.
- The authors define *equity* as "when intersections of social identities, residence in marginalized communities, and/or experience with oppressive systems do not determine opportunities, access to resources, and outcomes in life. Achieving equity requires

acknowledging, addressing, and dismantling systemic biases in mindsets, practices, and policies" (p. 4). Thus, equity for educators would entail holding antiracist and anti-oppression beliefs and considers how educational practice can mitigate inequities in terms of social justice.
- Third, the authors define *inclusion* as "anchoring the voices, perspective, and cultures of those most excluded from power and influence" (p. 3). Translating this to education requires educators to understand power dynamics to create an inclusive, collaborative learning environment.

These three definitions are central to understanding culturally responsive practices.

Defining Culturally Relevant, Responsive, and Sustaining Practices

Three main concepts that focus on culturally appropriate practices appear in the literature: culturally relevant, culturally responsive, and culturally sustaining practice. Some foundational principles cross all three but with slightly different emphases. Fundamental to all three are that educators should focus on student strengths rather than weaknesses, take an asset-based approach rather than use a deficit model, and take into consideration students' interests, contexts, and identities. These approaches prioritize improving the achievement of diverse students by connecting to their cultural orientations, diverse demographics, and learning styles. As Gorski (2016) notes, instilling an equity lens in education must focus on removing the conditions that have resulted in marginalizing students. These approaches address the cultural needs of communities and attempt to promote self-awareness about how to engage students from within the contexts of their communities (Khalifa et al., 2016). These approaches also address the social identities of students.

Ladson-Billings (1995) uses the term "culturally relevant pedagogy." This work has three foci:

- First, educational practice should yield success.
- Second, it should help students to develop a positive cultural identity while also yielding success through cultural competence.
- Third, practice should help students to recognize current cultural inequities through the development of critical consciousness.

Ladson-Billings stresses the importance of cultural competence and cultural integrity. This form of pedagogy focuses on critical competences and promotes high standards for all students.

Gay (2002, 2018) uses the term "culturally responsive teaching." This work capitalizes on students' performance styles, backgrounds, prior experiences, and cultural knowledge to make instruction relevant and meaningful. Gay's work also emphasizes examining inequities in students' personal experiences. According to Gay (2002), culturally responsive teaching uses "cultural characteristics, experiences, and perspectives of ethnically diverse students as conduits for teaching them more effectively" (p. 106). The author (2018) also supports empowering students through personal efficacy. Gay's work focuses on cultural competence, critical consciousness, and academic success. Gay (2018) outlines many recommended steps to enhance instruction. I summarize the most relevant. First, it is important for educators to examine their own beliefs and expectations about different demographic groups. They should model culturally diverse values and listen to diverse students. Educators should advocate for their students and create partnerships with students and shared responsibility. Educators should admit to their fallibility. They should hold high standards and expectations for all students. Educators should understand how students learn and how their knowledge is organized. They should recognize that student performance entails more than test scores. They should acknowledge that experiences beyond the school walls affect what happens in school. Gay's list of strategies are sound dispositions or habits of mind for all teachers.

Paris (2012; Paris & Alim, 2014) uses the term "culturally sustaining pedagogy." The major emphasis in this work is that instruction should sustain students' cultures through empowerment. Such pedagogy focuses on components of students' cultures that are valued, helping students to embrace their own backgrounds. This perspective moves beyond relevance and responsiveness with the explicit goal of supporting multiculturalism (Paris, 2012). The work seeks to minimize stereotype threat by tapping students' social contexts and instruction that are relevant to their own lives. It stresses active learning, collaboration, and the provision of feedback to enhance improvement.

Other Related Research and Development

Other researchers also present concepts relevant to culturally responsive practice. Dover (2013, 2015) emphasizes the need to deal with oppression, inequity, and prejudice through using a social justice lens. Similarly, Beck (2020) espouses the notion that social justice is an amalgam of culturally responsive, relevant, and sustaining practice as well as humanizing pedagogy and asset-based approaches. Scheetz and Senge (n.d.) challenge educators to confront their own biases, which often are unconscious and are reinforced subtly by systemic issues. They promote creating a vision of how to address inequity for all children through examining educator beliefs and developing awareness.

Most relevant to the CRDL work is that of Gorski and Pothini (2018), who discuss how diversity and social justice impact educational practice, emphasizing the need for educators to be aware of how contextual conditions may impact students' educational experiences. They present compelling case studies intended to challenge educators' thinking in what they term "gray areas" of practice (p. 6). The cases encourage educators to take a broad view of situations while reflecting deeply on the conditions and disparities that underlie situations that they may face. Much like this volume, the authors take a systems perspective, discussing the complex interactions that may foment inequities in educational settings. They promote the idea of the opportunity gap rather than the achievement gap. They also consider educators' lack of equity literacy a barrier to good practice. For Gorski and Pothini, equity literacy consists of being able to recognize biases, respond to biases, redress biases, and create bias-free learning environments.

The connection between data and equity is prominent in the work of Safir and Dugan (2021) in what they title "street data." Street data are often qualitative data that reflect students' experiences. The authors emphasize assets that are culturally responsive. The focus of street data is to shift the paradigm for data use to equitable and sustaining learning. Similar to the systems perspective of Scheetz and Senge (n.d.), the focus here is on understanding underlying root causes or the "whys" to determine steps for more permanent fixes. According to Safir and Dugan, street data yield "systemic information about equity" (p. 57) through using feedback loops that provide educators with information to address students' needs. Their position is that such data are more likely than traditional data to reveal what is happening with students. The data can uncover and accommodate cultural differences, including language, learning styles, and relational norms. The authors contrast the more traditional data that lack context and nuance to discern such cultural differences. Traditional data typically assume a deficit model and may promote implicit biases. Street data align completely with the philosophy of CRDL.

Because assessment is such a fundamental part of educational practice, Taylor (2022) has presented the concept of culturally and socially responsible assessment. It is based on the three approaches noted above. Assessment that informs instruction must incorporate the philosophies and emphasize culturally responsive practices. The Branch Alliance for Educator Diversity (2021) also addresses bias in assessment. The organization notes that high-stakes assessments are used for sorting rather than for improving instruction. Such assessments must be free of bias, and educators must understand the importance of using multiple measures, not a single metric. Branch suggests several strategies for reducing assessment bias, including many of those noted in the data equity section of this chapter. For example, educators must avoid confirmation bias and confront their unconscious biases. They must consider alignment of the assessment to what is being measured. These are simply sound educational practices.

Moving from assessment back to classroom practices, the Branch Alliance (2021) has provided a relevant resource titled *A Primer on Inclusive Instruction*. In this resource, the organization lays out several competencies essential to the delivery of inclusive instruction. Some competencies for inclusivity are to

- question assumptions, biases, and stereotypes;
- consider intended and unintended consequences of instruction;
- consider who might be advantaged or disadvantaged by the instruction;
- determine what is known about students' cultures, both visible and invisible;
- examine marginalization, oppression, power structures, and privilege; and
- move away from deficit models to asset models.

Branch's competencies are what education would consider habits of mind or dispositions. They pertain to self-awareness, equity literacy, cultural competence, and sociopolitical clarity. The primer also addresses strategies for inclusive classroom climate. For example, it is important to celebrate successes, apply root cause analyses, engage in self-reflection, and practice mindfulness. Branch promotes social justice, safety, resilience, transparency, trustworthiness, collaboration, and empowerment. Branch also lays out strategies for an asset-based approach to instruction. Strategies include

- building mutual respect,
- challenging systemic inequities,
- holding high expectations,
- identifying students' lived experiences,
- building awareness of language use,
- letting students make mistakes as part of the learning experience, and
- providing formative feedback to capitalize on students' strengths and needs.

Exploring the Concepts

Muniz (2020) identified the competencies that are part of culturally responsive teaching. These competencies formed the basis of an examination of how culturally responsive teaching is displayed in state standards. The alignment to the standards is discussed in chapter 3.

- The first competency is to reflect on one's cultural lens. This competency requires the ability to introspect and consider one's own beliefs, biases, and stereotypes. It requires educators to consider how their own values shape their perspectives and influence their interactions with students and colleagues.
- The second competency is to recognize and redress bias in the system. This competency focuses on the ability to understand bias at different levels of the education system, from personal to institutional. It examines the extent to which educators' actions reinforce or redress actions that may create bias and disparities.
- The third competency is to draw on students' culture to shape curriculum and instruction. This competency relates to Shulman's (1986, 1987) knowledge of learners and their characteristics. It requires educators to understand students' cultural backgrounds, context, family situations, and their lived experiences. It requires structuring instruction to accommodate those background characteristics.
- Competency 4 is to bring real-world issues into the classroom. This competency asks educators to bring into their classrooms authentic events that may include social justice and discrimination as learning opportunities.
- Competency 5 is to model high expectations for all students. Similar to the DLFT disposition, the belief that all students can learn, this competency necessitates that educators hold high expectations for all students. It also requires educators to help students hold the same high expectations for themselves.
- Competency 6 is to promote respect for student differences. This competency is about helping educators and students reflect on student differences in terms of their cultures, experiences, contexts, and backgrounds.
- Competency 7 is to collaborate with families and the local community. This is about parental engagement and the need to develop trusting relationships based on family cultures and values.
- Competency 8 is to communicate in linguistically and culturally responsive ways. The style of communication matters, so it is important for educators to communicate in ways that reduce misunderstanding, trying to capitalize on cultural norms for communication, both verbal and nonverbal.

Various states have promoted cultural responsiveness by creating frameworks that can guide educators to more effective practices. Take, for example, the Connecticut State Department of Education (n.d.), which produced a document that contains five key elements, the desired student actions, the needed classroom conditions, and supporting instructional practices. The elements include

- express care,
- challenge growth,
- provide support,
- share power, and
- expand possibilities.

The actions and verbs are telling. The document uses terms such as believe in me, hold me accountable, respect me, empower, inspire, advocate, encourage, and let me be heard. The classroom conditions are much like the competencies outlined by Muniz (2020): examine values, beliefs, and identities; use real-world issues; engage families and the community; and connect to students' contexts and backgrounds.

THE MERGER TO CULTURALLY RESPONSIVE DATA LITERACY

Motivating the Merger

The transition to CRDL from DLFT was motivated by several issues. Although DLFT was deemed important by many educators and professional organizations (Mandinach & Gummer, 2016a; Mandinach & Nunnaley, 2017), it failed to gain traction for a variety of reasons. Perhaps the biggest issue was the negativity around data use due to the focus on accountability data. The links between accountability data and the marginalization of vulnerable groups of students became a very real issue (Datnow, 2017; Datnow & Park, 2018). Recognizing that the outcome of data use in terms of high-stakes assessments was causing an equity issue motivated moving the discussion away from such data. I had been advocating for a broad definition of data for a long time, trying to impress upon the research and practice communities that data are more than test scores (Mandinach, 2012; Mandinach & Gummer, 2013, 2016b).

Assessment literacy has been addressed in educator preparation at least peripherally for decades. Districts sometimes seek professional development about new assessments or technologies to support them. However, the professional development is more technical; that is, how to access the data rather than how to use the data, or even questioning whether the data are the right data. Assessments certainly are a major source of educational data while data literacy has become an emerging need, moving the conversation to broader sources of data, more than test scores. Consequently, when we began work on data literacy in 2010, one thing we did was ask the data and professional development experts we convened the difference between data literacy and assessment literacy. The overwhelming response was that assessment literacy was a component of data literacy because assessments were only one form of data (Mandinach & Gummer, 2011). Yet the education field still viewed and views data narrowly. This issue became one of my guiding precepts but was met with much resistance.

The distinction between data literacy and assessment literacy looms large as students become more diverse and data sources proliferate. Conflating the two constructs is seen as a major misconception in the theory, research, and practice (Beck et al., 2019; Mandinach & Schildkamp, 2021). Some of the conflation relates to confusion about what are data. As noted here, data are more than test scores. The focus on such limited data and the use of assessment literacy, although important, constrains educators' ability to address the needs of all students and may perpetuate structural inequality. With a broader view of what data are and through data literacy, educators have the advantage of using a wide range of diverse data sources to gain a more comprehensive understanding of their students.

Here are two examples of the resistance or misunderstanding of the differences that cause conflation of the two constructs. First, books on data use, including some of my own, are typically categorized and promoted by publishers as assessment books—a total misrepresentation of the content. Second, I was asked to serve on a panel to help define how data and assessment literacy would be reflected in what would be newly developed assessments for certification by the National Board of Professional Teaching Standards. Board certification is a big deal, so having data literacy displayed prominently would be an important statement to allay the conflation. It would mean having an explicit statement that all data are informative and important. It did not happen.

Instead, the conflation persisted with assessment data being the pervasive and recognized data source that teachers needed. The test specifications included the term "assessment" to modify actions such as a teacher must know how to collect assessment data, analyze assessment data, and interpret assessment data. What was needed was to say use diverse data sources, not just assessment data. This was truly a missed opportunity to communicate to the professional community the need to look broadly at data. Instead, the sole focus remained on assessment data.

Broad data sources are essential to gain a comprehensive understanding of the whole child. These data sources move far beyond sorting, categorizing, and quantifying students by a single numerical metric. The data sources help to understand students beyond performance and cognition, considering motivation, affect, self-esteem, grit, interests, home context, and much more. Using CRDL means trying to understand not just the data but what is behind the data. Such variables are essential for educators to assume an asset model and an equity lens. These are some of the foundational precepts of CRDL and partly stimulated the merger of data use with culturally responsive practices.

Chronic absenteeism as a variable is an example of why CRDL is important. Absenteeism is related to many other variables of interest. For example, an educator may identify low-performing students based on their performance indices but not look past those metrics. However, performance has been linked to chronic absenteeism that can then lead to failure and ultimately, to a risk of dropping out (Barat et al., 2021, 2022). As Roig and Luna state (Barat et al., 2022), understanding the variable "serves as a stark reminder that chronic absence undermines efforts to increase educational equity for students from populations historically underserved and marginalized in our school system" (p. 1). Clearly, taking a CRDL approach can help educators move beyond the obvious to the root causes and complex interactions that may impact students.

Beyond moving the focus away from accountability to diverse data sources, CRDL differs from DLFT in at least one fundamental way. CRDL explicitly emphasizes culture and equity. One of DLFT's dispositions is the belief that all children can learn, but it is not explicit about the role of equity and culture, although it is implied in the disposition. DLFT also is not explicit in promoting an asset-based model, whereas it is a foundational precept of CRDL. Moving the data conversation toward an asset model that focuses on the whole child with an equity lens has become increasingly important as students become more diverse and are challenged with events such as the pandemic. Yet, we know that the focus on helping educators to become both data literate (Mandinach et al., 2017; Mandinach et al., 2015) and culturally responsive (Muniz, 2019) is limited. State standards and credentialing requirements do not adequately address these constructs. This issue will be discussed in chapter 3.

Defining CRDL

Having discussed the rationale to transform thinking toward CRDL rather than the more limited DLFT, I now provide a working definition of the construct. CRDL combines the two key concepts—culturally responsive practices and data-driven decision making—to better enable educators to develop and implement equitable instruction and other educational practices. CRDL is defined as the ability to use diverse sources of student data and other key data literacy skills to inform decision making about the whole child, using an equity lens and asset-based model to better serve the needs of all children. More specifically, it is the ability to transform information into actionable knowledge by collecting, analyzing, and interpreting diverse data (student performance, socio-emotional, motivation, home context, health, justice, interests, etc.) to help determine instructional steps or inform other educational decisions while taking particular note of the context, background, interests, strengths, and surrounding information of students that may affect their performance and behavior (Mandinach et al., 2019). CRDL entails "(a) seeking a broad range of data sources about students as learners in schools, as humans with personal histories, and as children with unique experiences and identities; and (b) identifying and interrogating bias in analysis and interpretation of the information they collect and using those understandings about students to design learning experiences, choose instructional materials, and implement appropriate interventions as necessary to support student learning" (Mandinach et al., 2019; Warner, 2021, p. 2).

Warner (2021) identifies five foundational components to CRDL:

1. The belief that all students can learn.
2. The use of race-conscious pedagogies and recognition of the role of race and how it may influence decision making in education.
3. The use of a cycle of inquiry that can uncover biases and challenge assumptions.
4. The use of diverse data sources.
5. The need to collaborate to develop and implement actionable strategies.

Note the interplay of these components with those in DLFT and the explicit focus on equity.

To be clear, part of the objective of CRDL is to use a broad lens in terms of diversity and inclusion beyond race and ethnicity, an intersectionality about diversity that is nuanced. Students are complex and present with many demographic and background characteristics. Thus, CRDL must take into consideration a broad scope of variables that include gender, sexuality, class, language learner status, poverty, migration status, economic status, homelessness, foster care, military designation, religion, ability, and political leanings, among others.

The Guiding Questions

As we began to think about how to communicate CRDL to educators, we developed the concept of using guiding questions intended to prompt thinking about students and their contexts using three topical or information domains (Mandinach et al., 2019). The idea was to push the focus beyond just academics to the whole child. The domains included academic performance and schooling experiences, personal story and experiences, and examining and interrogating bias. The focus of these guiding questions is to use many sources of data to understand students and to reflect on the potential biases that may impact educational practice. The intent of each of the domains is for educators to consider probing, thought-provoking questions that can lead to insights about their students that might go unnoticed or ignored. There are more than 100 questions across the three domains, far too many to address here. Instead, I will provide examples, subsumed within the overarching categories.

The academic performance and schooling experiences domain focuses on questions about student performance and experiences that students encounter while in school. The general topics and some examples include:

- Academic performance
  - What do you know about the students' academic outcomes in school?
  - Has the student succeeded academically in the past?
  - Does the student succeed on assignments, projects, and other class activities?
  - Does the student do relatively well on quizzes, tests, and standardized tests?
  - Is the student's performance relatively consistent?
  - Does the student seem to grasp the ideas and content presented in class on the first try? Second try? Multiple tries? Does not grasp it at all?
  - Are there certain content areas where the student excels?

- Are there certain content areas where the student struggles?
- What are the student's favorite subjects? Least favorite?
- What form of instruction best suits the student?
- Behavior
  - What do you know about the student's behavior in school?
  - Is the student respectful toward other students? Teachers? Administrators? Others?
  - Does the student have consistent attendance? Frequently absent or tardy?
  - Does the student come to class prepared (i.e., brings required materials, completes homework and assignments)?
  - Does the student pay attention in class?
  - Is the student disruptive in class?
  - Does the student show interest in learning?
  - Does the student show excitement and curiosity toward learning?
  - Does the student exhibit persistence?
  - How does the student handle frustration about low performance, failure, or negative feedback?
  - Is the student able to reflect on his or her own performance?
  - Does the student require extra help?
  - What are the student's academic expectations and aspirations?
  - Does the student do any extracurricular activities? Belong to any clubs?
  - Does the student participate in sports and/or on teams?
- Classification and special services
  - Is the student classified by any special designation and/or receiving special services?
  - Is the student identified as gifted and talented?
  - Is the student labeled as special education?
  - Is the student identified as an English language learner?
  - Is the student eligible to receive free and reduced meals?

The personal story and experiences domain focuses on students' lives outside of school, including their home situations and self-identity. Some of the questions include:

- Family
  - What do you know about the student's family?
  - Who are the legal guardians of the student (biological parents, guardians who are relatives, guardians who are not related, foster parents, other)?
  - Is the student adopted?
  - Are the parents divorced or divorcing? Is the process acrimonious or stable?
  - Are the parents involved in the student's education?
  - Does the student have siblings? Older? Younger? Are other relatives residing in the same home with the student? Are others (nonrelatives) residing in the home and with the student?
  - What is the language spoken in the home by parents/guardians/family members?
- Living conditions
  - What do you know about the student's living conditions outside of the school?
  - Does the student and family live in a homeless shelter?
  - Does the student live in an enriched environment or a dangerous environment (e.g., gang violence, high crime, subject to domestic violence)?
  - Does the student have access to books or other educational resources at home?

- Does the student have access to WiFi at home?
- How does the student get to and from school each day (i.e., public transportation, school bus, walk, ride from parents/guardians)?
- Is there evidence that the student does not have sufficient food at home?
- Has the student changed schools frequently?
- Does the student work? If yes, to help support the family? Earn spending money?
- Health
  - What do you know about the student's physical health?
  - Is there evidence that the student has persistent health issues?
  - Is there evidence that the student does not get sufficient sleep?
  - Does the student have an eating disorder?
  - Does the student appear to have appropriate hygiene (washed, brushed, clean teeth, brushed hair)?
  - Does the student smoke?
  - Is the student pregnant? A parent?
  - Is the student a cutter or show signs of doing bodily self-harm?
- Social and emotional
  - What do you know about the student's social and emotional health and well-being?
  - Does the student seem happy, sad, distressed, angry, or something else?
  - Is there evidence that the student has been bullied?
  - Does the student have body image issues or abnormalities, such as severe obesity, excessive hair, crossed eye, wears glasses, hearing aids, etc.)?
  - Does the student have friends? Is the student part of a clique? Is the student a loner?
  - Does the student exhibit any sources of anxiety or psychological distress?
  - Interactions with justice system: What do you know about the student's interactions, either formal or informal, documented or undocumented, with the justice system?
  - Has the student experienced serious behavioral issues that have resulted in an arrest?
- Identity
  - What do you know about the way the student self-identifies?
  - Is English the student's first language? If not, what is the student's native language?
  - Has the student identified as LGBTQ?
  - Is there any reason to believe that the student is struggling with gender identity issues?
  - Does the student belong to a religious group?
  - Does the student belong to a political group?

The third domain is examining and interrogating bias. This domain is essential and is intended to stimulate deep introspection among educators. Everyone has some sort of bias, based on preconceived notions, experiences, stereotypes, or some other rationale. The questions are intended to be edgy, making people even feel uncomfortable as they consider their beliefs. The questions ask educators to consider how they view their students and how biases may influence their classroom practices and decisions. The questions are about beliefs, conscious or unconscious, as well as actions based on those beliefs. Because these questions are central, I present all that we developed.

Do you believe that

- All students can learn?
- "One size fits all" is an effective instructional strategy?
- Whatever you do for the students who struggle the most won't make a difference?

- Gifted students do not need as much help as other students?
- Boys are out of control more than girls?
- Girls are innately worse at math than boys?
- Asians are innately better at math and science and just plain smarter?
- Introverted students are not smart?
- Students with disabilities can learn?
- A student with an individualized education program (IEP) or 504 plan will struggle?
- Students with limited English language proficiency cannot learn?
- Standardized tests may not adequately reflect the knowledge and skills that some of your students have?
- Students' home lives or community are inhibiting their academic potential?

Do you:

- Focus only on the "bubble kids" to the exclusion of students on the extremes?
- Celebrate student achievements?
- Take personal interest in your students beyond their academic performance?
- Show respect for cultural diversity? Ethnic diversity? Religious diversity?
- Show respect for those whose political leanings differ from your own?
- Allow your students to discuss and exhibit their cultural, ethnic, religious, political, and gender identities?
- Penalize a student who is absent for a religious holiday?
- React differently to a student who is a "jock"? LGBTQ? See a student with a head scarf, a yarmulke, or a cross? See a seemingly thin or obese student? Receiving free and reduced meals?
- Differentiate instruction?
- Adapt your teaching to students' different learning styles? Cultural styles and forms of expression? Learning differences and special needs?
- Assume that students with limited language proficiency are problematic for you as a teacher?
- Group your students by ability?
- Arrange your classroom to accommodate students with disabilities?
- Tolerate subtle forms of bias in the classroom?
- Promote non-bullying practices?
- Discourage offensive language and actions? Patterns of informal discrimination, segregation, or exclusion of members of specific groups from school clubs, committees, and other school activities? Exclusionary activities among students?
- Allow other students to make fun of students because they are different?
- Reflect on the root causes of a student's behavior or performance?
- Take into consideration the home circumstances of your students?
- Find ways to engage parents, regardless of their backgrounds and means?
- Find alternative ways to assign homework if some of your students lack connectivity at home?
- Value the unique characteristics that students bring to the classroom?
- Try to listen with an open mind to all students and colleagues, even when you don't understand their perspectives or agree with what they are saying?
- Consider how things you say might be hurtful to a student or subsets of students?

- Assign certain students harsher consequences for the same behavior and academic infractions?

Have you:

- Taken specific action to dispel misconceptions, stereotypes, or prejudices that members of one group have about members of another group at your school?
- Evaluated your materials to ensure that they do not reinforce stereotypes and are fair and appropriate?

Do you teach to:

- Remediate a problem of practice?
- Capitalize on students' strengths?
- Capitalize on students' interests?
- Capitalize on students' cultural backgrounds?

Many of these questions, especially the ones about bias, are used as the basis for the scenarios that appear in chapters 4 and 5. Grounding the scenarios with these questions hopefully will stimulate users' thinking about their own practices and how they think about their students, or not, based on their characteristics, their personal histories, and their prior academic performance. Additional questions educators might consider are:

- How do you judge your students and based on what characteristics?
- What characteristics or variables are most important to you in making decisions?
- Do you think you are judging your students fairly and accurately?
- Are there impediments to fair judgment? If yes, what might they be?
- How might you overcome such impediments?
- Are there policies in your school that facilitate or impede fair and equitable practices?

Chapter 3

Setting the Landscape for the Scenarios

This chapter sets the stage for the scenarios presented in the next two chapters. The scenarios can be used in educator preparation programs and by professional development providers. They can also stand alone for personal self-education. The scenarios provide authentic situations from which to learn about the application of CRDL. Before presenting the scenarios, however, it is important to lay out how CRDL is embedded in standards for the field of education. The standards provide guidance to users about where and how CRDL relates to key skills required by state agencies and professional organizations that educators must display or that must be included in educator preparation programs. This chapter also provides guidance from documents produced at the federal level that promote data use.

WHAT THE STANDARDS SAY

Several types of resources provide guidance about how states, professional organizations, and other relevant agencies address data literacy and culturally responsive practices. These agencies identify skills, knowledge dispositions, and behaviors to be requirements for educators. They provide guideposts to educator preparation programs, credentialing agencies, and technical assistance providers about the essential skill sets educators need to use data effectively and appropriately. I review here the relevant documents and identify the specific standards that relate most closely to CRDL and to the scenarios that follow in the next two chapters.

InTASC

The Interstate Teacher Assessment and Support Consortium (InTASC) produced the *Model Core Teaching Standards and Learning Progressions for Teachers* (CCSSO, 2013), which consists of ten standards and learning trajectories. The standards pertain to topics such as instruction, assessment, and content knowledge. Each standard is categorized into three sections: performances, critical knowledge, and critical dispositions. The standards also include learning progressions that lay out how the components are manifested with increasing expertise.

Analyses of state standards indicate that states increasingly are adopting the InTASC standards or parts of them (Mandinach et al., 2015; Mandinach et al., 2017). In 2014 only a small number of states had adopted InTASC; a few years later, more than half the states had adopted them, and an increasing number (42 states and the District of Columbia) more recently. Many of the components align to DLFT, if not explicitly mentioning data, then by extrapolation. Frankly, the standards are more aligned to assessment literacy than data literacy, but the latter certainly can be inferred.

Because a large number of InTASC components are found to relate to CRDL, I summarize here the general topics.

In Standard 1, Learner Differences, and Standard 2, Learning Differences, the focus is for teachers to understand learners' characteristics such as languages and dialects, giftedness, family and personal backgrounds, and disabilities to design instruction. The standards stress the importance of tapping learners' assets, interests, and needs.

Standard 3, Learning Environments, focuses on designing environments that support engagement, instruction, and learning.

Standard 4, Content Knowledge, and Standard 5, Application of Content, focus on how content can be reflective of multiple representations.

Standard 6, Assessment, is perhaps most closely aligned to DLFT and CRDL due to assessments being one form of data. It also reflects on one of the issues for data literacy, the conflation with assessment literacy. This standard pertains to the knowledge of how to measure learners' progress to inform instructional decisions. This standard also incorporates different types of assessments that align to learners' needs, thereby reflecting the whole child perspective.

Standard 7, Planning for Instruction, and Standard 8, Instructional Strategies, focus on how to develop instruction that can address learners' needs, assets, and backgrounds.

Standard 9, Professional Learning and Ethical Behavior, relates to how teachers' practice provides engaging experiences to meet the needs of all learners, including the personal identities of students.

Standard 10, Leadership and Collaboration, focuses on the importance of students' and families' beliefs, norms, and cultures.

Clearly, not all InTASC standards directly relate to CRDL, but those that highlight the importance of instruction, assessment, and practice that address the needs of diverse learners are particularly relevant. The collection of data and information, therefore, can be fed back to improve responsiveness of practice.

Model Code of Ethics for Educators

The National Association of State Directors of Teacher Education and Certification (NASDTEC, n.d.) developed the *Model Code of Ethics for Educators* (MCEE), which lays out the general principles considered necessary for the ethical practice of education. Ethics is a fundamental precept in educational decision making to promote the need to use data both effectively and appropriately (Mandinach & Gummer, 2021). Ethics gets to the heart of addressing the needs of all learners while redressing potential biases and harm. Therefore, the MCEE is relevant here.

When Mandinach and Gummer (2021) extended the data literacy work to the examination of data ethics, they found that prior versions of the MCEE contained very little about data use. The most recent version of the MCEE (NASDTEC, 2023) now contains content fully aligned to DLFT and CRDL. The MCEE discusses ethical decision making; the responsible use of data, research, and evidence; and the use of data to inform practice. It addresses the need to take into consideration students' characteristics such as age, gender, context, beliefs, and backgrounds. Beyond protecting the privacy and confidentiality of student data, the MCEE mentions the appropriate use of technologies and the potential misuses of social media and cyberbullying. Perhaps most important to CRDL, the MCEE explicitly outlines the need for cultural sensitivity.

State Standards: Data Literacy

Mandinach and colleagues (2015) and (2017) conducted in-depth analyses of how state standards reflect data literacy. Documents that could be located from each state were examined for the presence of skills that pertain to data use. States were diverse; some states were steeped in skills and knowledge that relate to using data effectively, and others had a dearth or total lack of attention to data. A few states even had explicit data standards. The states that adopted the InTASC standards, by default, address many data-related skills. At least one state (Arizona), requires all educator preparation programs to complete a checklist of how their curricula address data literacy. North Carolina has an entire document devoted to the importance of data literacy. Virginia, one of the early adopters, integrated data literacy across its standards.

Of specific relevance to CRDL is that many states conflated assessment literacy with data literacy, with an obvious focus only on the use of assessment data. Mandinach and Gummer (2016b, 2016c) make clear that data literacy is a much broader construct than assessment literacy and was, in part, the motivation for the transformation of DLFT to CRDL, ensuring that educators know how to use diverse data sources to better understand their students. Data literacy broadens the focus for educators on the whole child rather than relegating them to be reflected only as student performance indices However, because assessment is so central to educational practice, most, if not all state standards explicitly focus on assessment literacy from which data literacy can be extrapolated.

A similar focus could be found among the revised assessments for board certification of teachers. Instead of broadening their focus on what data board-certified teachers need to use to inform their practice, the focus sadly (in my opinion) remains solely on assessment data. For example, board-certified teachers must know how to examine, analyze, and interpret assessment data. The key here is using the term "assessment" to modify data. It constrains the definition of what data are. It sends a message to the education community that the only data that matter are those from assessments. In my opinion, as well as others in the data field, this is a myopic position and a missed opportunity to emphasize diverse data.

As noted in the prior chapter, the result of Mandinach and Gummer's (2016a, 2016b) development of the DLFT construct yielded more than 50 knowledge, skills, and dispositions. In the transformation to CRDL, a subset of those skills aligns more with the data literacy component than with the cultural responsiveness component.

SLDS Data Use Standards

The SLDS (Statewide Longitudinal Data Systems) Support Team (2017) consisted of a group of educators from local and state education agencies who collaborated to produce a set of standards that specified the knowledge, skills, and professional behaviors for data use. These standards validated the knowledge, skills, and dispositions that Mandinach and Gummer (2016a, 2016b) laid out for the DLFT construct.

- The Knowledge Standard describes topics such as data assumptions, data limitations, ethics, privacy, measures, data quality, and data processing.
- The Skills Standard highlights planning, selecting, collecting, analyzing, interpreting, communicating, and acting.
- Professional Behaviors include ethical use, rules and regulations, collaborations, and continuous improvement, much like Mandinach and Gummer's dispositions.

These standards fall squarely on the data side of CRDL and do not address cultural responsiveness or equity. The Support Team's goal for these standards was for the document to serve as a guide for preservice and in-service settings to inform about data literacy. The standards also were generic for all educators, mostly those individuals responsive for data in a school or district.

CULTURALLY RESPONSIVE TEACHING: STATE STANDARDS REVIEW

Much like the work by Mandinach and colleagues (2015; 2017), Muniz (2019) undertook an analysis of state standards to determine whether and how culturally responsive teaching (CRT) was represented. Muniz also took the perspective that if the concept was represented in the state standards, it would reflect that CRT was an essential state priority that educator preparation programs should and must address. Muniz considered the three main theories: culturally responsive (Gay, 2018), culturally relevant (Ladson-Billings, 1995), and culturally sustaining (Paris, 2012) practices. The general findings of the examination showed that although CRT was present to some degree among the standards, it was not explicit or well-defined. It included no trajectories of learning like those outlined in the InTASC Standards. The report stated that "the majority of the states do not yet provide a description of culturally responsive teaching that is clear or comprehensive enough to support teachers in developing and strengthening their CRT practice" (p. 8).

The analysis examined the extent to which the standards addressed eight competencies described in chapter 2:

- reflect on one's cultural lens
- recognize and redress bias in the system
- draw on students' culture to share curriculum and instruction
- bring real-world issues into the classroom
- model high expectations for all students
- promote respect for student differences
- collaborate with families and the local community
- communicate in linguistically and culturally responsive ways

The analytic strategy used to examine the state documents was similar to what Mandinach and colleagues (2015; 2017) used. Muniz (2019) also noted the relevance of the InTASC Standards (2013), particularly to avoid bias.

The findings were also similar to data literacy findings; some states were better at incorporating CRT in their standards but not very explicit about the specifications. All states had some references to CRT but failed to address the full scope of the eight competencies. All states addressed Competency 7 and almost all addressed Competencies 3, 5, and 6. Fewer states addressed Competencies 1, 4, and 8. A highlighted finding was that only three states explicitly confronted institutional bias; the analysis also noted that Washington and Alaska have stand-alone standards for CRT.

Further Guidance From Two Federal Documents

As the emphasis on data use was taking hold, the Institute of Education Sciences (IES) produced a series of documents that examined the research literature for evidence about various topics. The practice guide on data use (Hamilton et al., 2009) was one of the earlier reports. The panels culled more than 3,000 documents, which ultimately yielded five recommendations that still are relevant for effective data use and data literacy:

1. First, data use is a cyclical process leading to instructional improvement. As discussed in the prior chapter, data-driven decision making is an iterative process. Just because a decision is reached does not mean that you are finished.
2. Second, educators should help their students become data-driven decision makers. This entails getting students engaged in their own data so that they understand their progress and learning goals.
3. Third, schools and districts must establish a clear vision for data use. Educators should be given guidance on how and why data are to be used. This issue relates to the accountability versus continuous improvement dichotomy.
4. Fourth, and most relevant to development of data literacy, is the creation and support of a data culture. Data cultures provide for much-needed professional development and technical assistance to build human capacity for data use. Data cultures provide for data coaches, data teams, dedicated collaborative time, and other supports needed for effective data use.
5. The final recommendation is to have data systems to support data use. In 2009, the report spoke of data systems. Now, years later, technologies have expanded significantly to support data use well beyond data warehouses. Dashboards, apps, and other technologies now make possible data use and data access unimaginable a decade ago.

The National Forum on Education Statistics, a branch of IES, produces guides that relate primarily to data use. The guides are written mostly by staff from state and local education agencies, although other contributors can be involved (I represent the Regional Educational Laboratory West as an author). One of the most recent guides is on data literacy, which the Forum has deemed important. The Forum Guide (2024) is intended to help education agencies understand how to promote data literacy among staff and other stakeholders. Paraphrasing the guide, using data accurately and ethically is important when considering the assumptions people make about what data mean. The guide states, "Without data literacy, people may struggle to interpret and apply data accurately, leading to ineffective use or misinterpretations of data" (p. 12). Clearly, data ethics and assumptions loom large here. The guide promotes an asset model and addresses the whole child through data use. It describes appreciative inquiry as a method for approaching data through an asset model and mitigating implicit bias.

The guide discusses several topics critical to data literacy, some of which are beyond the scope of this volume. It discusses the need for educators to understand data quality, data governance, data privacy, metadata, and data visualization. It then describes the need to develop data cultures, much like the IES practice guide. First is the need to build the capacity of educators (as well as other stakeholders—school boards, community) to know how to use data. The guide is clear that data literacy must be a priority for education agencies. Educators must have easy access to the needed data. Educators must be transparent in how they use data. Educators must have dedicated time and support for data use. They must understand educational data and must communicate using the data. The guide promotes the use of diverse data sources, a primary tenet of CRDL.

The guide then describes how to build data literacy by targeting key skills. Educators must be able to understand data analytics and must know how to interpret results. They must know how to use data effectively and ethically to inform their practice. They must be able to communicate with data. These resonate with key skills, knowledge, and dispositions of DLFT and CRDL. The guide also includes a self-assessment.

The guide provides recommendations for creating a positive data culture, one in which there is a trusting environment rather than one of shaming and blaming. A key to this culture is building educators' capacity to use data through sustained, ongoing professional development and technical assistance. The guide promotes the idea of helping educators gain capacity through an onboarding process. It also emphasizes the importance of transparency, strong leadership, an explicit vision, and a commitment to data use.

CONCLUDING THOUGHTS

Clearly more work needs to be done to explicitly highlight the importance of both cultural responsiveness and data literacy among professional standards. Part of the issue is accepting a common definition of both concepts. This becomes a systemic issue that begins with including the concepts in the standards that then leads to educator preparation programs including them in their curricula, which then extends to in-service experiences, not just preservice. The concepts need to be fundamental across educators' careers and reinforced at every juncture.

Laying out how data literacy and CRT are displayed in professional standards and requirements provides the foundation for the scenarios presented in the next two chapters. Most of the scenarios address a subset of the standards and can assist users in grounding the relevance of each scenario in authentic situations that educators may face.

Chapter 4

Introduction to the Scenarios

A PRIMER, USER'S GUIDE, AND THE FIRST SET OF SCENARIOS

This chapter provides scenarios of possible situations educators may face in their practice. Each scenario reflects an authentic situation that requires the application of CRDL skills, knowledge, and dispositions. The scenarios are grounded in the guiding questions developed for the Regional Educational Laboratory Program (Mandinach et al., 2019). These questions, as outlined in chapter 2, focus on three topical areas:

1. academic performance and schooling experience,
2. personal story and experiences, and
3. examining and interrogating bias.

In particular, the scenarios focus on unconscious bias. They are meant to push users to reflect deeply about assumptions, beliefs, and biases they may have about students who present with certain characteristics. To be clear, the intent here is to *not* perpetuate stereotypes but, rather, to force users to confront possible perceptions that may lead to unconscious prejudices.

Because of the sensitive nature of some of the scenarios, I have tried not to stereotype any demographic group of students or educators. To that end, the names used are those of pets of friends, tennis partners, and colleagues, so the scenarios cannot be accused of portraying any specific demographic group in a negative manner. It is hard to think negatively about a husky versus a French bulldog, a mutt versus a purebred, or a cat versus a dog or even a camel!

Another comment about the scenarios: they are meant to be generic. In many cases, the situation could occur at any level and in any course. For some scenarios, however, the situation may be specific to a course (e.g., physical education or mathematics) or a grade level. I have also taken note about a gender balance for the characters; that is, not all teachers are portrayed as female or administrators as male, similarly with the students.

A final caveat pertains to the data highlighted in the scenarios. I have made an explicit effort to ensure that student performance indices are not the primary data source for many of the scenarios. Because one precept of CRDL is using diverse data sources to inform decision making, the scenarios address many different forms of data, some of which hopefully will stimulate creative thought about how best to gain a comprehensive understanding of the whole child.

THE STRUCTURE OF THE SCENARIOS

The scenarios have been developed in a flexible format that can be integrated into preservice coursework, in-service professional development, or for self-instruction. They can be used as a stand-alone assignment or activity, for in-class discussion, and for individuals or small groups. The scenarios were developed in a way that an instructor or professional development provider can use them in their entirety or extract portions. Additional materials can be added to enhance the applicability of the situation.

The scenarios were developed to address a range of topics and issues in which CRDL and a whole child perspective should enhance decision making. Topics are sometimes embedded in a content domain and grade level, but they should be able to be generalizable. Each scenario has been developed with a consistent structure intended to help users maximize information and understanding. The structure has been used elsewhere to teach about data privacy (Mandinach et al., 2023). Two differences: each data privacy scenario includes specific references to standards because of their unique features and had specific guidance about data privacy regulations. The scenarios here are much broader and reflect the standards addressed in the prior chapter. Each scenario has been written to stand alone, although there are similarities in certain sections. Instructors should select the scenarios most relevant to their course content or objectives. The scenarios include the following sections:

Learning Objectives. The scenario begins by explicitly laying out the targeted knowledge and skills that it is intended to stimulate. The learning objectives can be linked to professional standards. The objectives are written at a high level of generality but specifically reflect why CRDL is important to the decision-making process.

Scenario Narrative. This section provides a scenario that depicts a situation that educators are likely to experience in their practice. The situation is intended to be as authentic as possible. It requires the use of CRDL to address potential biases to consider the ethical dilemma and effective actions. For the most part, the scenario requires the user to consider what data (often more than student performance indices) are needed to understand the situation and the context. The scenarios are intended to stimulate thinking about the whole child, equity, and an asset model.

Discussion Questions. This section presents general questions that an instructor or professional development provider can pose to students to consider foundational issues about the scenario.

Extending Activities. This section can be used to dive more deeply into the nuances of the scenario. These activities can be used for group discussions in class, extended assignments, or technical assistance. They require a more thorough consideration of the situation.

From the Evidence Vault. Where possible, research studies are cited that relate to the specific situation. The research-based references can provide insights into how evidence has been applied to similar situations.

In the News. As a researcher, it is sometimes frustrating to note that topics often appear in public and social media before a research base has been established or those in practice have been made aware. Mandinach and Gummer (2021) noted this in examining data ethics. Educators also have commented about finding out key information about students or their family through social media or on the news before there is any discussion about an issue in class or in school. This section taps media sources that present related reports where possible. Some scenarios have been motivated by articles that appeared in the media.

Teaching Notes. This section is intended to help instructors, providers, and other users make effective use of the scenario. It lays out considerations about the dilemma and how instruction should be handled. For some, this section may not go far enough in terms of guidance for use. Given that professors and technical assistance providers are experienced in their areas of expertise, I leave some of the more nuanced discussion possibilities to them, especially those most engaged in actual practice. Such individuals may develop alternative and creative uses that I have not considered.

Ethics. At the foundation of CRDL is the objective that educators should approach practice from a whole child perspective, use an asset model, and invoke an equity lens. Ethics comes into play when educators face dilemmas about the use of data and their ensuing actions. This section notes possible ethical issues that may arise, given the specific situation. This section also addresses the impact of CRDL on ethical decision making where possible.

References and Resources. This section guides users to relevant materials for a deeper dive into the topic.

FINAL GUIDANCE

As a final explicit statement about the scenarios, to be clear, it is my intention not to insult anyone or show bias in any way. There is no intention to offend or stereotype. The scenarios are intended to be as authentic as possible. I have tried to tap into different categories from the unconscious bias section of the REL Guiding Questions. The scenarios cover a full range of demographics, characteristics, and special status.

As users work through the scenarios, it will be helpful to consider foundational questions that focus squarely on CRDL:

- Using a CRDL approach, what data sources will be helpful to you in addressing the situation?
- How would the data you need differ if you were to not use CRDL?
- How might your analytics differ?
- How might your interpretations differ?
- Does using a CRDL approach impact the actionable steps you might take?
- How does a CRDL lens impact or inform your perspective on the scenario?
- How might you view the scenario differently if you were using a deficit model versus an asset model?

These questions form an essential mind-set for approaching the scenarios. They set up a dichotomy in which the educator or student applies or fails to apply CRDL skills, an equity mind-set, a whole child perspective, and an asset approach. The key is how diverse data sources are being used, or not. Does the user move beyond student performance indices? Does the user consider important contextual information? Does the user look beyond the obvious? Does the user let confirmation or implicit bias influence the examination, analysis, and interpretation of the data? These are important factors for instructors or technical assistance providers to consider when observing the approach to and interpretation of each scenario.

The scenarios are presented in the remainder of this chapter and in the following chapter. Because a wide range of issues is addressed, there is no easy way to sort or categorize them. The scenarios often deal with equity and ethics where preconceived assumptions can lead to inaccurate interpretations; that is, unconscious or conscious bias. They deal with diversity in student characteristics such as culture, religion, gender identity, and poverty. They address students with special status designations such as giftedness, homelessness, military family, foster care, and language learner. They address various kinds of home circumstances such as adoption, divorce, abuse and neglect, and parental behaviors. Some scenarios deal with student behaviors such as bullying and justice issues. Some scenarios deal with educators' behaviors that may be less than ethical, such as gaming the system.

I urge users to scan the topics and extract those scenarios that seem most aligned to your courses or professional development and your interests. The titles are intended to indicate the content, but in some instances, intended twists in the plots require more nuanced treatment. The first 18 of the 39 scenarios are presented below.

FIRST HALF OF THE SCENARIOS

Military Family
Food Insecurity
Home Circumstances
Transportation Challenges
Falling Asleep
Sheltered
Unhoused
Transportation
Disheveled
Inconsistent Performance
Learning Differently with Support
Gifted
Outing
Adoption
Confirmation Bias
Jocks
Sibling History
Facial Recognition

MILITARY FAMILY

Learning Objectives

- Understand the unique issues surrounding children from military families.
- Appreciate that children from military families have had transient, disjointed academic histories.
- Understand that children from military families may experience anxieties and concerns because of a parent or family member deployed or in harm's way.
- Appreciate how knowledge of a military student's special status may impact interactions with that student.

Scenario Narrative

Bennett is a high school junior at Turbo High School. His mother is deployed abroad on a naval vessel. Because of the family's military status, Bennett has already attended several schools in various states. There have been disruptions to the continuity of his academic coursework, but as a diligent student, he has tried to keep up. Sometimes Bennett struggles as the curricula have differed.

In addition, Bennett has struggled to make connections with other students because of the frequent moves. It has been difficult for him to establish lasting friendships because of the transient nature of the family.

Ms. Ava is one of Bennett's teachers. She has been monitoring Bennett's performance. Sometimes Bennett seems current with what is being taught; at other times, he seems not to have the foundation for the topic. Ms. Ava also has noticed that Bennett sometimes sits alone in the cafeteria while the other students sit together at tables.

Scenario 1. Administrators and teachers at Turbo are aware of Bennett's military designation and are making every effort to accommodate for his academic history.

Scenario 2. Administrators and teachers are not aware of Bennett's military designation.

Discussion Questions

1. What actions should Ms. Ava and the educators take to accommodate the special status?
2. How might the data point of military family be used to assist the educators in being more effective and responsive to Bennett's needs?

Extending Activities

- Discuss which data may indicate that Bennett is struggling and how those data might be used to assist him.
- Discuss how knowledge of Bennett's military designation can inform practice.
- Discuss how the military designation might impact a student in terms of academics, socially, and emotionally.
- Discuss how this scenario might differ if educators are not aware of Bennett's military designation. Without that data point, how might this impact how educators interpret the same performance and behavioral indices?

From the Evidence Vault

Neil, L. (2015). The unique needs of students from military families. *BU Journal of Graduate Studies in Education, 7*(1), 50–53.

In the News

Biden, J. (2016, April). *Operation Educate the Educators: Recognizing and supporting military-connected students through university-based research, community partnerships, and teacher education programs.* Invited speech at the annual conference of the American Educational Research Association, Washington, DC.

Teaching Notes

Military designation, as a special status indicator, is often overlooked or not even made available in many school districts' data systems. Because of the uniqueness of a military family, awareness of the designation can help educators be responsive to the needs of military students. Military children often move from post to post, causing gaps in their academic histories. They experience little permanence, which also impacts their ability to establish lasting friendships. This may be especially difficult, depending on age and grade level. Socio-emotional well-being also is affected. Military students may exhibit anxiety over the safety of the parent or family member, especially if the serviceperson is deployed or in harm's way. Anxiety can manifest itself academically, socially, behaviorally, and emotionally. At the very least, educators should be aware of the potential impact for such students.

Take, for example, the fact that Ms. Ava notices that Bennett sometimes sits alone for lunch. This might indicate isolation, loneliness, or that other students have not accepted Bennett. The observation could lead to a discussion with Bennett about his well-being. The varied performance could also indicate issues that Ms. Ava could address with Bennett. Careful examination of where his learning strengths might be but also where he might have missed foundational skills due to the family moves might be informative.

Ethics

Without knowledge of military status, educators might make inaccurate assumptions about a student. The interpretation of behavior, emotions, performance, motivation, or something else make be very different knowing or not knowing about the context of the student. Having access to the designated data point can explain a great deal about the student, leading educators to more effective and meaningful interactions. Without such access, educators' perceptions of the situation may likely be skewed.

If the educators at Turbo are unaware of Bennett's military status, interpretation of his behavior, performance, and socio-emotional well-being would likely be different. With such knowledge, the educators can better understand the impact of the many moves on Bennett's academic career as well as his anxiety, social behavior, and emotions.

References and Resources

IES. (2022, May). *Active-duty military families and school supports.* Inside IES Research: Notes from NCER & NCSER. https://ies.ed.gov/blogs/research/post/active-duty-military-families-and-school-supports

FOOD INSECURITY

Learning Objectives

- Understand the need to look beyond the obvious explanations and surface level data to better understand the student.
- Understand the importance of not jumping to conclusions before doing a deeper dive into contextual data.

Scenario Narrative

Layla is a student at Polo Elementary School. She has been a diligent student and is well liked. One day, Layla is spotted entering the faculty lounge and emerges with a lunch bag. It is also reported that Layla was seen stealing food from other students. She gets reported to building leadership, who asks her to come in for a talk. Mr. Barnaby, the principal, tries to get to the bottom of the situation before punishing what is apparently a behavioral issue. After all, Layla was seen stealing. But is she really a thief? After further investigation, Mr. Barnaby uncovers some distressing evidence. Yes, Layla did take the lunches. However, the explanation provides context for the actions. He discovers that there is little food at Layla's home. The family has few resources, and she simply is hungry. She had not eaten in days. Layla suffers from food insecurity.

Discussion Questions

1. How should Mr. Barnaby handle the situation?
2. What would Mr. Barnaby do if the theft was simply a behavioral issue, not something more?

Extending Activities

- Discuss which data would best inform Mr. Barnaby's investigation.
- Discuss how using a CRDL approach provides a more comprehensive perspective to this scenario.
- Consider how conclusions and actions might differ had Mr. Barnaby not discovered Layla's food insecurity.
- Discuss what actions Mr. Barnaby might take to assist Layla and her family. What other data might be needed to better inform these actions?

From the Evidence Vault

Atwood, E. D., Jimerson, J. B., & Holt, B. (2019). Equity-oriented data use: Identifying and addressing food insecurity at Cooper Springs Middle School. *Journal of Cases in Educational Leadership*, 1–16. https://doi.org/10.1177/1555458919859932

In the News

Qiu, L. (2023, January). Families struggle as pandemic program offering free school meals ends. *New York Times*. https://www.nytimes.com/2023/01/22/us/politics/universal-school-meals-free-lunches.html

Teaching Notes

All too often in education and elsewhere, individuals rush to judgment based on an initial, mostly superficial observation or information. Such superficial and incomplete information may skew interpretations and lead to inaccurate conclusions and inappropriate action steps. A more considered approach is likely to yield a more complete and accurate depiction of the situation. It would provide a deep dive into root causes and possible explanations. This is the case with Layla. Simply attributing her actions to a behavioral problem fails to uncover the true causes, which goes to home context and familial circumstances. After Mr. Barnaby discovers the situation in Layla's home, he could meet with her parents and work with appropriate social service agencies to help provide them with needed assistance. This would be the humane course of action, based on looking at multiple sources of information, rather than taking the limited view.

Ethics

Examining limited data can be problematic. It can skew interpretations and subsequent actions. The rush to conclusions can be completely inaccurate. The ethical course of action is to do one's due diligence. Look for root causes. Examine or consider alternative explanations, not just the obvious. Weigh the evidence and base the decision on multiple sources. Consider the ramifications or potential harms of limited examination. Consider how using a CRDL approach provides a more complete and accurate depiction of situations that may be much more complex than at first view.

References and Resources

Rural Health Information Hub. (n.d.). *Approaches to addressing food insecurity in school settings.* https://www.ruralhealthinfo.org/toolkits/sdoh/2/economic-stability/food-insecurity

HOME CIRCUMSTANCES

Learning Objectives

- Consider what contextual factors might contribute to students' performance or behavior.
- Understand that although academic indices may be central, many other data points can provide valuable insights into patterns of performance or behavior.

Scenario Narrative

Mr. Houdi has been an educator for many years. He has seen students come and go. He has taken a deep interest in the well-being of his students. In turn, students respect Mr. Houdi and often confide in him. Mr. Houdi also is an astute observer and recognizes changes in patterns that can mean that something is happening in a student's life.

Buster is a seventh-grade student. Mr. Houdi had Buster in his homeroom last year. But this year, Mr. Houdi has observed something different with Buster. His behavior is "off." Something is not quite right. He is concerned. Mr. Houdi approaches some of Buster's current teachers who report that his academic performance has had some swings from quite good to troublesome. Buster has also exhibited emotional swings. Mr. Houdi is now increasingly concerned. He asks Buster for a chat in which Buster admits that things are difficult at home. His parents have been fighting a lot and are contemplating divorce. It is impacting everything in Buster's life.

Discussion Questions

1. What do you think of Mr. Houdi talking to other teachers about Buster and the other teachers reporting to him about Buster's performance and behavior?
2. Do teachers who no longer have a student have the right to discuss that student?

Extending Activities

- Discuss the kind of "investigation" or data collection about Buster that Mr. Houdi undertook.
- Discuss the extent to which educators can and should share information about a past or present student to better understand that student.

From the Evidence Vault

Vance, A., & Waughn, C. (2021). Turning to data ethics to resolve FERPA's modern questions. In E. B. Mandinach & E. S. Gummer (Eds.), *The Ethical Use of Data in Education: Promoting Responsible Policies and Practices* (pp. 56–66). Teachers College Press.

Teaching Notes

Educators who collaborate in data, grade, or content teams often exchange information about students to try to better understand their performance. They exchange instructional strategies to help students succeed. Mr. Houdi is a concerned educator, who through astute observation (a form of data collection) recognized that something is happening with Buster. He can choose to ignore the observations or collect additional information that can lead to insights into what is occurring with Buster. There is likely to be a fine line between prying and ignoring. But if a student's well-being is at risk, it might be necessary to ascertain the basis of the root causes of the situation.

Ethics

How much information is too much information? Does a former teacher have a right to interject and investigate what is happening with a former student? Who has the right to ask and know? Does a former teacher have the right to ask current teachers for information? Are those teachers allowed to provide the requested information? To what extent are teachers allowed to have discussions and share information about students? These questions go to the heart of data ethics. Regulations control the protection of data privacy and confidentiality. And there are requirements around being a mandated reporter. Educators must balance students' rights with helping students who potentially are in challenging situations.

References and Resources

Scheid, M. (2019, November). The educator's role: Privacy, confidentiality, and security in the classroom. *Student Privacy Compass*. https://studentprivacycompass.org/scheid1/

TRANSPORTATION CHALLENGES

Learning Objectives

- Consider different explanations based on diverse data sources.
- Learn not to jump to conclusions based on one initial data point.

Scenario Narrative

Ms. Rosie is a teacher at King High School. She teaches mathematics, primarily algebra to sophomores and juniors, and is the department chair. She has a student, Enzo, who rarely makes it to his first period class, often arriving mid-class or even later. Students at King are allowed a certain number of tardy days before they are penalized. Further, because algebra has a definite trajectory of learning and impact on subsequent math classes, the activities Enzo misses are fundamental to this class as well as future classes. Ms. Rosie is afraid Enzo will continue to fall behind. Ms. Rosie is somewhat frustrated by this issue and is struggling to determine the appropriate actionable steps. She commutes, and other students can get to school on time, so why not Enzo?

Her first reaction is to report Enzo to the office for the persistent tardiness. But she resists and decides to discuss the situation with him. He needs to understand the consequences of his actions. Ms. Rosie does a 180. Instead of being frustrated, she is now concerned after talking with Enzo. She learns that Enzo was moved recently to a group foster home that is not served by the bus schedule. It is too far for him to walk or ride a bike. The foster family cannot drive him to school, so he is left to fend for himself, mostly using public transportation. He must transfer several times, and if he misses a connection, he is delayed. Relying on public transportation is risky but Enzo's only option. Ms. Rosie sees that Enzo is making the effort to get to school, not oversleeping or slacking off. This information completely changes her perspective of the situation.

Discussion Questions

1. What would the outcome have been had Ms. Rosie used only the tardiness data indicator to draw a conclusion about Enzo?
2. Should Ms. Rosie have explored deeper to better understand the situation?

Extending Activities

- Discuss how looking at the fuller picture through different data sources impacted Ms. Rosie's perspective on Enzo's situation.
- Discuss what steps Ms. Rosie can take to help Enzo get to school on time or help him catch up with the class.
- Discuss whether it might be viable for the school to modify Enzo's class schedule to accommodate his transportation challenges.
- Discuss whether the interpretation would be different if Enzo were found to be unhoused rather than in foster care; if he were living with his natural family.

From the Evidence Vault

Chingos, M., & Blagg, K. (2017). *Student transportation and educational access.* https://www.urban.org/research/publication/student-transportation-and-educational-access

In the News

Mitchell, C. (2020, July). Solving the student-transportation conundrum. *Education Week.* https://www.edweek.org/leadership/solving-the-student-transportation-conundrum/2020/07

Teaching Notes

Clearly Ms. Rosie has taken an interest in understanding Enzo's situation and is helping to find a solution to the problem. At first blush, it was an apparent case of tardiness, when in fact, the situation was much more complex. Some educators may have chosen to focus only on the academic impact of the tardiness—that Enzo consistently was late and fell behind on the course content. Ms. Rosie could have chosen simple strategies to help Enzo catch up, but she sought the root cause where there might be work-arounds to mitigate the problem. One strategy might be to adjust Enzo's schedule to a study hall in first period, which is less consequential than a class. She might work with school authorities to find other solutions for alternative transportation. Awareness of the problem could lead to solutions.

Ethics

Discussing the situation with Enzo helped the data gathering process that can lead to a more balanced and evidence-based decision. Without the full picture, Ms. Rosie likely would have drawn an inaccurate conclusion that would have unintended and harmful consequences for Enzo.

References and Resources

Accredited Schools Online. (2022, November). *Transportation solutions for students.* https://www.accreditedschoolsonline.org/resources/transportation-in-college-and-on-campus/

FALLING ASLEEP

Learning Objectives

- Learn to look at many contextual factors to understand students' performance and behavior.
- Learn to recognize anomalies or outliers for students that may indicate an issue.

Scenario Narrative

Mr. Fonzie is a math teacher at a Josephine High School, which is in a low-income, urban area. The math department faculty members pride themselves on motivating students and engaging them through activities such as a math team or math club. Mr. Fonzie loves seeing his students succeed, and many of his students have received prestigious scholarships to attend college.

One student, Ivy, has been a favorite. Ivy has always excelled. She has been an excellent student and has exhibited promise in math competitions. But lately, Mr. Fonzie has noticed that Ivy looks exhausted. A couple of times she has fallen asleep in class. She gets her homework in, but it is not as thorough as in the past.

Mr. Fonzie is concerned. He does some investigating through discussions with other students and teachers. He discovers that Ivy's father recently was incarcerated, leaving Ivy to take after-school jobs to help support the family. Mr. Fonzie tries to find a way to help Ivy and to protect her prospects for receiving a much-needed scholarship.

Discussion Questions

1. Do you think that Mr. Fonzie is overstepping the bounds?
2. What actions do you think are appropriate for Mr. Fonzie to take?

Extending Activities

- Discuss how Mr. Fonzie has collected data about Ivy beyond observing her academic performance to try to determine what may be causing the changes in behavior and performance.
- Discuss what kinds of action steps Mr. Fonzie might take to provide possible assistance for Ivy.

From the Evidence Vault

Qureshi, M. S., & Ahmad, A. (2014). Effects of father absence on children's academic performance. *Journal of Educational, Health and Community Psychology, 3*(1), 1–6. https://core.ac.uk/download/pdf/295346373.pdf

In the News

Tillotson, M. C. (2014, November). How schools can help disadvantaged families. *IFS*. https://ifstudies.org/blog/how-schools-can-help-disadvantaged-families

Teaching Notes

Dramatic changes in students' performance or behavior can indicate something happening in their lives. Especially when a teacher has established a meaningful relationship with a student, it is not unheard of to make an inquiry. The student can choose to answer or not. Directly asking friends or other teachers is also possible within reason and without violating the student's privacy. Such inquiries must be made with sensitivity and caution. Discretion is needed, especially if the situation can embarrass the student. In Ivy's case, she is being asked to carry a heavy load, juggling jobs to help support her family while trying to maintain academic rigor. Having understanding teachers can provide some flexibility and accommodations for the student. Possible solutions may also be sought from social services to assist the family.

Ethics

There is a delicate balance between prying into sensitive areas and obtaining useful information that can help educators assist a struggling student. Various data points can provide indications of a student's situation. Triangulating those data can provide the school with possible strategies to help not only the student but the family as well.

References and Resources

Student Training & Education in Public Service. (n.d.). *Resources & support for students with challenges at home.* https://www.publicservicedegrees.org/resources/students-with-family-challenges/

SHELTERED

Learning Objectives

- Gain an understanding of home context and how important that information is to address students' needs.
- Learn not to make assumptions about students' home circumstances.

Scenario Narrative

Ms. Lu is a teacher at Gizmo School District. Every year before school begins, Gizmo leadership asks the elementary school teachers to conduct informal home visits for all incoming students. The district has funding for this work. The purpose of these visits is for teachers to introduce themselves to the students and their parents or guardians and establish rapport. Teachers meet with the family for 30 minutes or so and just talk to get to know one another. No notes are taken. Teachers basically are collecting invaluable data about the student and home circumstances based on observations.

Ms. Lu visits one student, Lexie, and learns that she, her siblings, and their mother reside in a shelter to protect against domestic abuse. A few other of Ms. Lu's students reside in homeless shelters. Ms. Lu takes in this information and realizes that the home situations of these students is an important data point that will impact how she structures her assignments and can help devise strategies and accommodations to better meet the needs of Lexie and the other sheltered students.

Discussion Questions

1. How does knowing about a student's home circumstances help a teacher to adjust practice?
2. What do you think about home circumstances as a data point?

Extending Activities

- Discuss how knowing that a student is homeless, sheltered, or in foster case may inform a teacher's practice.
- Discuss what you think of the practice of home visits for gathering information about students.

- Discuss how you can use this sort of information to inform what you do to better address the needs of your students.

From the Evidence Vault

George, J. (2014, February 4). Remarks made at the Data Quality Campaign's Empowering Teachers with Data: Policies and Practices to Promote Educator Data Literacy, Washington, DC.

In the News

Edmentum. (2021, November). *Understanding the challenges faced by homeless students: What educators can do to help.* https://blog.edmentum.com/understanding-challenges-faced-homeless-students-what-educators-can-do-help

Moore, J. (2013). *Research summary: Teaching and classroom strategies for homeless and highly mobile students.* https://nche.ed.gov/wp-content/uploads/2018/11/res-summ-teach-class.pdf

Teaching Notes

Ms. Lu is fortunate to have the opportunity to meet with her students and their families to establish rapport and gain invaluable information that will help her better meet the needs of these students, given their living circumstances. Knowing that a student resides in a shelter, is homeless, is in foster care, has come from an abusive environment, or other relevant home circumstances can provide helpful information so the teacher can make accommodations or modifications to practice. For example, maybe the shelter has limited WiFi. Knowing that connectivity may be a problem can influence the type of assignments given. Knowing that a student may not have a quiet place in which to study can be informative. Teachers then can seek strategies and work-arounds to help the students.

Ethics

Because of the sensitive nature of some home circumstances, teachers should be mindful about sharing information with others. Administrators likely are aware that a student resides in a shelter, is in foster care, or in a protected house safe from abuse, but this information should not be readily shared unless there is an educational need to know.

References and Resources

District of Columbia Public Schools. (n.d.). *Family engagement.* https://dcps.dc.gov/node/994252

Hallett, R. E., & Skrla, L. (n.d.). *Supporting students who are experiencing homelessness.* https://www.aft.org/ae/spring2021/hallett_skrla

Mehrotra, S. (2021, October). Understanding students and their families who are experiencing homelessness or housing insecurity during a pandemic. *Education Trust.* https://edtrust.org/the-equity-line/understanding-students-and-their-families-who-are-experiencing-homelessness-or-housing-insecurity-during-a-pandemic/

UNHOUSED

Learning Objectives

- Recognize the special needs of unhoused students.
- Understand how data can help educators address the need of challenged students.

Scenario Narrative

Mr. Chester is a librarian at Smudge High School in a large urban area. This urban area has many struggling students. There are absent parents and many unhoused students. In the library, Mr. Chester has a closet that has an extensive collection of food and clothing for students in need. The students are aware of this, and they trust Mr. Chester and look to him for assistance. Notably, students visit Mr. Chester on Friday afternoons to receive a backpack of food so that they will have sustenance over the weekend. This is essential for the survival of many students.

The backpacks are part of a formal program, but Mr. Chester has taken it upon himself to find funding to provide clothing. Informal donations help support Mr. Chester's program, but he always needs more. To obtain funding, he needs to provide concrete data about the number of students he is serving. Collecting such data while maintaining the privacy of the students is very important. Mr. Chester is aware of the need to maintain students' trust, yet he also must continue to seek the needed support to sustain his program.

Discussion Questions

1. How should the school handle the unhoused students?
2. Does Mr. Chester's approach make sense?

Extending Activities

- Discuss the practice of weekend backpacks.
- Discuss how you would handle people who may question the provision of supplies for unhoused students.

From the Evidence Vault

Kurtz, M., Conway, K. S., & Mohr, R. D. (2020). Weekend feeding ("BackPack") programs and student outcomes. *Economics of Education Review*, 79. https://doi.org/10.1016/j.econedurev.2020.102040

In the News

Cameron, C. W. (2017, August). Backpack programs help schoolkids combat hunger on weekends. *Atlanta Journal-Constitution*. https://www.ajc.com/lifestyles/food--cooking/backpack-programs-help-schoolkids-combat-hunger-weekends/bMkfl7NRxVBY45zdAk4NZO/

Cooper, C. A. (2016, May). How school backpack programs help alleviate hunger in America. *U.S. News & World Report*. https://health.usnews.com/health-news/blogs/eat-run/articles/2016-05-24/how-school-backpack-programs-help-alleviate-hunger-in-america

Teaching Notes

Many schools and districts now provide programs to help unhoused or needy students. Backpacks provide essential food for students who may otherwise go hungry over the weekend. What Mr. Chester is doing is compassionate and important. A key, though, is how to identify students if they do not self-identify and then how to gain the trust in the program. Finding sustained funding for such programs establishes the importance of the program to maintain continuity of support for the students in need.

Ethics

A major issue is how to obtain the sensitive data about students' status as homeless, unhoused, or in need. Educators must protect the privacy of the students due to the sensitive nature of their situations. They need to triangulate data sources and seek assistance with social agencies that might be able to position special services and support for the students.

References and Resources

A number of sources online in specific regions describe local backpack programs.

Feeding America. (n.d.). *Backpack program.* https://www.feedingamerica.org/our-work/hunger-relief-programs/backpack-program

Feed More. (n.d.). *Backpacks for nourishment.* https://feedmore.org/our-work/hunger-relief-programs/weekend-backpacks/

TRANSPORTATION

Learning Objectives

- Understand the importance of thinking creatively about potential data sources beyond student performance indices.
- Recognize the need to dig more deeply into different data sources to find root causes of issues.

Scenario Narrative

The Bradley School District is in a rural area. Most students must take buses or personal vehicles to school. Administrators at Bradley have noticed a curious trend, with a subset of students struggling on assessments and other assignments. Data teams meet to try to understand what is causing this performance issue. They look at the usual suspects in terms of data, but they continue to be stumped. Nothing seems to be an apparent cause for these students. One educator gets an interesting idea. Ms. Elena hypothesizes about students whose commutes are especially long and are stuck on the school buses for an hour or so. Administrators admit that they had modified the bus routes recently and some students' commutes increased significantly. Sure enough, further investigations yield a relationship between commute time and performance. Administrators at Bradley therefore decide to reexamine the bus schedule as well as considering other solutions such as installing WiFi on the buses, with the expectation that this would help students complete their homework assignments.

Discussion Questions

1. What kinds of variables might educators examine to discover root causes?
2. Why is it important to look beyond performance indices?

Extending Activities

- Discuss the advantages of casting a wide view of potential data sources to uncover root causes.
- Discuss what kinds of actions Bradley can take upon learning of the trend data.

From the Evidence Vault

Cattagni, A., & Farris, E. (2011, May). *Internet access in U.S. public schools and classrooms: 1994–2000* (NCES Statistics in Brief). https://nces.ed.gov/pubs2001/2001071.pdf

In the News

Dillon, S. (2010, February). WiFi turns rowdy bus into rolling study hall. *New York Times.* https://www.nytimes.com/2010/02/12/education/12bus.html?searchResultPosition=2

Liberman, M. (2021, April). Most students now have home internet access but what about the ones who don't? *Education Week.* https://www.edweek.org/technology/most-students-now-have-home-internet-access-but-what-about-the-ones-who-dont/2021/04

Teaching Notes

Looking beyond performance data for causes and possible relationships can be useful. Insights from diverse sources of data can provide creative ideas that lead to solutions. In the case of the transportation data, there have been instances in which such investigations have led to modification of bus schedules or installing WiFi on buses, with the expectation that students will have access to enable them to do their homework. One district did install WiFi but with interesting unintended consequences. The expectation was to provide connectivity for students. Instead, drivers reported a decrease in behavioral issues on the buses. Students may or may not have been doing homework, but at least they were not physically fighting. Other districts have parked WiFi-enabled busses in low-income neighborhoods to provide hubs for students living in those communities. This was another solution to helping students to complete their work. So, be mindful of creative solutions and unintended consequences.

Ethics

Decision making requires due diligence and oftentimes, out-of-the-box thinking to develop creative solutions. Educators should not rush to snap judgments and interpretations based on limited data. The triangulation of diverse data sources often leads to creative solutions. It is important, therefore, to be open to examining multiple data sources from which to discern patterns and ultimately solutions, even if the ideas may seem outlandish.

References and Resources

Internet Society. (2017, November). *Internet access and education: Key considerations for policy makers.* https://www.internetsociety.org/resources/doc/2017/internet-access-and-education/ and https://www.internetsociety.org/resources/doc/2017/internet-access-and-education/

DISHEVELED

Learning Objectives

- Learn how to identify a student who may be struggling with some sort of crisis, based on different sources of data.
- Learn how to look for warning signals through different media to identify a student in crisis.

Scenario Narrative

BW is a fifth-grade student at Willow Elementary School. He is usually an outgoing, upbeat person. He engages with his classmates and interacts politely. In the past couple of weeks, BW has come to school with what best could be called disheveled clothing. His clothes are wrinkled and often dirty. They do not fit properly and are sometimes torn. It does not look like he has had a shower in a while either. BW has not said anything to friends or teachers and continues as usual. Mr. Cujo is concerned and is unsure how to proceed to determine what is happening with BW. He wonders if he should call BW's home. He wonders whether to ask BW's best friend, Lilly, if she knows if anything is going on.

Discussion Questions

1. What actions should or can Mr. Cujo take?
2. Should Mr. Cujo call BW's home or speak to Lilly?
3. What data might he collect?

Extending Activities

- Discuss what, if any, might be the boundaries around gathering student data about a student's well-being beyond the school wall?
- Discuss some reasons for BW's appearance and what might or should be done about it.

From the Evidence Vault

Erickson, M. F., & Egeland, B. (2002). Child neglect. In J. E. B. Myers, L. Berliner, J. Briere, C. T. Hendrix, C. Jenny, & T. A. Reid (Eds.), *The APSAC Handbook on Child Maltreatment* (pp. 3–20). Sage.

In the News

Murphy, S. (2022, August). Pandemic showed teachers' key role in spotting child abuse. *U.S. News and World Report.* https://www.usnews.com/news/health-news/articles/2022-08-09/b-8-11-pandemic-showed-teachers-key-role-in-spotting-child-abuse

Teaching Notes

There are times when situations in students' homes impact what happens in school. Indicators of problems can be readily apparent. For example, a student who is unclean or wearing dirty, torn, or ill-fitting clothing can be signs of neglect at home. Perhaps the family does not have power. Perhaps the family is having financial difficulties. Perhaps a parent or guardian is indisposed. Whatever the explanation, these are obvious indications that the student may not be provided for at home and the situation should be investigated.

Ethics

Educators must be alert to warning signs of possible neglect or trauma. Such indicators can provide evidence that something is happening in a student's home that may require intervention by seeking appropriate social services. Observing educators should share their suspicions with leadership, who can alert the proper social services agencies to obtain the needed assistance for the student or the family.

References and Resources

Child Welfare Information Gateway. (n.d.). *Recognizing child abuse and neglect: Signs and symptoms.* https://www.childwelfare.gov/pubPDFs/signs.pdf

INCONSISTENT PERFORMANCE

Learning Objectives

- Learn to look beyond student performance indices to detect issues that might be affecting a student.
- Learn to take a whole child approach.

Scenario Narrative

Ms. Cookie is a high-school science teacher. She works closely with her students to help them get through challenging content and then apply to college and for scholarships. She takes an interest in her students. One student, Ellie, has begun to concern her. Ellie has been absent a lot. Her performance has been inconsistent. She is usually a good student who gets her assignment completed in a timely manner. Because of the attendance issue, Ms. Cookie reaches out to Ellie's guardian, her uncle with whom she lives. Through the uncle, Ms. Cookie learns that Ellie is undocumented and fears that her status will be discovered.

Discussion Questions

1. What should Ms. Cookie do to help Ellie?
2. To whom can Ms. Cookie turn for guidance?

Extending Activities

- Discuss what responsibilities educators have when they discover that a student is undocumented.
- Discuss whether knowledge of this status should make a difference in a teacher's actions.

From the Evidence Vault

Murillo, M. A. (2017). The art of the reveal: Undocumented high school students, institutional agents, and the disclosure of legal status. *High School Journal, 2*(Winter), 88–108.

In the News

Jordan, M. (2022, June). A decade after DACA, the rise of a new generation of undocumented students. *New York Times.* https://www.nytimes.com/2022/06/15/us/daca-dreamers-immigration-reform.html?searchResultPosition=4

Teaching Notes

Laws protect undocumented students and provide them access to public education in the United States. Therefore, Ellie has the right to obtain education. Ms. Cookie has the right to teach Ellie. This does not mean that Ellie does not experience anxiety with a fear of possible deportation for herself or other family members. Ms. Cookie is astute to notice concerns and apprehension that is being manifested by inconsistent performance and attendance. Ms. Ellie can work with school administrators and social services to help protect Ellie and provide strategies to help enhance her educational experiences.

Ethics

Knowledge of Ellie's immigration status should be contained to individuals with a need to know. Violating Ellie's privacy and confidentiality could place her, her uncle, and family at risk. Therefore, Ms. Cookie can use her knowledge of Ellie's status to inform her actions and help the student, but the information should not be shared broadly. CRDL comes into play here through triangulation of data points and the display of awareness of and sensitivity to Ellie's home context. Ms. Cookie is taking a whole child approach to helping Ellie.

References and Resources

Immigrants Rising. (2022, September). *Overview of undocumented students.* https://immigrantsrising.org/wp-content/uploads/Immigrants-Rising_Overview-of-Undocumented-Students.pdf

NASSP. (n.d.). *Undocumented students.* https://www.nassp.org/top-issues-in-education/position-statements/undocumented-students/

LEARNING DIFFERENTLY WITH SUPPORT

Learning Objectives

- Recognize the interactions among different variables such as performance, self-esteem, and behavior.
- Understand that there may be creative solutions to solving students' learning challenges that can be informed by triangulating diverse data sources.

Scenario Narrative

Max is a shy third grader who has struggled with reading. He is embarrassed to read aloud in class as he is afraid to make mistakes and be perceived by other children as stupid. Each day when Mr. River convenes reading groups, Max withdraws. The first thing Mr. River notices is Max's reluctance to participate. His behavior is impacting many things, including his self-esteem and interaction with other children. He also notices indications that Max might have a reading challenge. Mr. River starts to collect data to better understand what is happening with Max. He also discusses Max with colleagues during the third-grade team meeting. Max may need glasses, or is there another issue?

Mr. River decides to try something with Max. He is aware that Max loves animals. The Hemmingway School District occasionally has used reading assistance dogs to try to strengthen students' reading skills. Reading assistance dogs have been shown not only to improve reading skills but also to enhance students' self-esteem and confidence. Mr. River introduces Max to Cooper, a lovable golden retriever, and the two of them go to "work."

Discussion Questions

1. What do you think of Mr. River's solution?
2. What do you think about how Mr. River collected different data?

Extending Activities

- Discuss how Mr. River used various data points to help find a solution to Max's challenges.
- Discuss the idea of reading assistance animals and their impact not just on performance but also confidence and self-esteem.

From the Evidence Vault

Hall, S. S., Gee, N. R., & Mills, D. S. (2016). Children reading to dogs: A systematic review of the literature. *PLOS ONE.* https://journals.plos.org/plosone/article?id=10.1371/journal.pone.0149759

Lenihan, D., McCobb, E., Diuba, A., Linder, D., & Freeman, L. (2016). Measuring the effects of reading assistance dogs on reading ability and attitudes in elementary school childhood. *Journal of Research on Childhood Education, 30*(2), 252–259.

In the News

London, K. B. (2021, July). What happens when kids read books with dogs. *The Wildest.* https://www.thewildest.com/dog-lifestyle/reading-dogs-benefits-children

Nussbaum, D. (2006, August). At these readings, listeners growl for more. *New York Times*. https://www.nytimes.com/2006/08/13/nyregion/nyregionspecial2/13njlibrary.html

Pearson, C. (2022, June). Why dogs can be so healing. *New York Times*. https://www.nytimes.com/2022/06/15/well/family/therapy-dogs-kids-stress.html

Teaching Notes

Reading assistance animals have become a creative strategy for helping struggling students. Schools, libraries, and bookstores are now using dogs and cats to help such students. Students read to a furry, cuddly creature who makes no negative comments or judgments about the student's reading ability. The student learns to read without negative feedback and in doing so, the process builds confidence and self-esteem. The student also gets to interact with a nonjudgmental, adoring animal. It is a win-win situation.

In this scenario, Mr. River triangulated data sources to find a strategy he thought would assist a struggling student. It was creative and addressed both the cognitive and affective components he observed in the student.

Ethics

This scenario depicts a case where the teacher used sensitivity to a student's learning challenges to find a creative solution. Mr. River capitalized on Max's interest in animals to find a research-based solution that might help Max with his struggles in reading as well as his self-esteem and confidence. Mr. River used different data sources to address the situation. He might have focused only on the reading behavior without considering Max's withdrawal and reluctance, or the converse. But he chose to triangulate data sources and took an asset-based approach to help Max. Bringing in a reading-assistance dog was brilliant as it focused on Max's interest and thereby helped him to feel more comfortable and ultimately improve his reading skills.

References and Resources

Intermountain Therapy Animals. (n.d.). *Reading education assistance dogs (R.E.A.D.)*. https://therapyanimals.org/read/

Noble, O., & Holt, N. (2016). A study into the impact of the Reading Education Assistance Dogs scheme on reading engagement and motivation to read among Early Years Foundation-Stage children. *International Journal of Primary, Elementary and Early Years Education, 46*(3), 277–290.

GIFTED

Learning Objectives

- Gain an understanding that student performance indices, especially standardized test scores, may not tell the whole story about a student.
- Understand the need to examine diverse data sources.
- Understand the need to treat the whole child.
- Consider that some groups of students may be under-identified through cultural bias.

Scenario Narrative

Ash is a student at Wayne Elementary School. Although Ash chronologically should be a first-grade student, all signs lead to her testing at a much more advanced grade level, particularly in mathematics. Simply put, Ash is gifted. Ash does enter first grade, and clearly she is more advanced than any other student. After a few weeks of school, the teacher, Ms. Oliver, asks Ash to "help" other students with their assignments so she will not get bored. The other students appreciate the help for the most part, and she forms strong bonds with them.

Ms. Oliver discusses Ash with her principal, Ms. Bhindi. Ms. Bhindi insists that Ash should be placed in a magnet school that specializes in gifted and talented students to maximize her potential. Ms. Oliver is not so certain this is the best course of action because her observations indicate that Ash simply wants to be one of the gang. She wants friends, not just to excel academically. Ms. Bhindi calls Ash's parents, Mr. and Mrs. Bruce, to advocate for Ash's transfer to the magnet school, which would position her with other extremely talented students who may or may not be the same age. During the subsequent meeting, Ms. Bhindi lays out the rationale for the transfer. The Bruces look to Ms. Oliver for her opinion because she has worked with Ash since the beginning of the school year and has observed her in the classroom. Ms. Oliver politely disagrees and stays relatively silent. The Bruces recognized Ash's gift a long time ago, but they also want her to be diverse in her interests, lead a "normal" life, and have social activities with her peer group—that is, basically be a regular but smart child.

Discussion Questions

1. Who do you think should make the decision about Ash's education?
2. What do you think about the differences between the teacher and the principal?
3. What role should the parents have in the decision?

Extending Activities

- Discuss what you see as the benefits and detriments of transferring Ash or having her stay in the original school. What would you do if you were the teacher? The principal? The parents?
- Discuss whether educators should consult with Ash about her preferences. Would it be different if Ash were older?
- Discuss whether academic performance should outweigh all other considerations.
- Watch the movie *Gifted* and discuss the portrayal of the educators and the family. What do you think about the perspectives taken by the principal, the teacher, the guardian, the grandmother?
- Discuss how differently the scenario might play out if Ash were not deemed gifted but were having a learning challenge that required a special placement. How different would the decision-making process be and what data would be involved in the analyses?
- Discuss how some groups of students may not be identified appropriately as gifted due to cultural bias, definitions of giftedness, or screening techniques for giftedness.

From the Evidence Vault

Munn, R. U., Ezzani, M. D., & Lee, L. E. (2020). Culturally relevant leadership in gifted education: A systematic literature review. *Journal for the Education of the Gifted, 43*(2), 108–142.

Rinn, A. N., Plucker, J. A., & Stocking, V. B. (2010). Fostering gifted students' affective development: A look at the impact of academic self-concept. *TEACHING Exceptional Children Plus, 6*(4), 1–13.

In the News

The movie *Gifted* deals with this exact situation. Portrayal of the characters provides insights into some of the nuanced issues.

Barnett, B. (n.d.). Advice for nurturing gifted & talented children. *OKCFamilyNews*. https://www.metrofamilymagazine.com/advice-for-nurturing-gifted-talented-children/

Brown, S. W., Renzulli, J. S., Chen, C-H., et al. (2005). Assumptions underlying the identification of gifted and talented student. *Gifted Child Quarterly, 49*(1), 68–79.

Gussner Elementary. (n.d.). *Nurturing your gifted child—Tips for parents*. https://www.jamestown.k12.nd.us/gussner-es/tag-talented-and-gifted/nurturing-your-gifted-child-tips-for-parents

Teaching Notes

Education should be about enhancing the potential of all students across the ability spectrum. Sometimes the most gifted students are ignored, with a focus instead on children who need more attention. Talent should be nurtured but not at the expense of other aspects of a student's life. Here, Ash just wants to be a normal kid, one of the gang, and to be accepted. That is important to her. It is important to discuss the balance of priorities to enhance the whole child. It is also important to provide options to the parents, as ultimately it is their decision about what they think is right for their child. Sometimes educators will disagree. The child may disagree as well. This scenario raises several key issues that are ripe for discussion, especially balancing academic needs with socio-emotional well-being.

Ethics

A consideration here is whose perspective takes priority. Certainly, identifying extreme talent and finding ways to nurture that gift are important. But at what point does socio-emotional well-being take precedence over academics? Leaders and teachers can express their expert opinion based on data and experience, but ultimately the decision rests with the family, taking into consideration the advice of educators. Families may or may not agree with the advice. Providing options based on individual data and evidence of best practice can facilitate informed decision making for all interesting parties.

But what happens if education experts disagree? What happens if the parents or even the student disagree with expert advice? As portrayed in the scenario, taking a whole-child perspective may be an essential component of sound decision making. Educators may see only the giftedness, not taking into consideration the context and the socio-emotional well-being of the student. Academics are only a subset of data points needed to make a comprehensive decision. A delicate balance needs to be made based on diverse sources of data to determine the best course of action. Further, consider the implications of how giftedness is defined and assessed. A cultural component to it may lead to a cultural bias, thereby leading to under-identifying some groups of students.

References and Resources

The movie *Gifted*.

Davidson Institute. (2021, November). *Attaining health and well-being through balance: Gifted parenting and strategies.* https://www.davidsongifted.org/gifted-blog/attaining-health-and-well-being-through-balance/

Hadaway, N., & Marek-Schroer, M. F. (2010). Multidimensional assessment of the gifted minority student. *Roeper Review, 15*(2), 73–77.

Marsh, H. W., & Parker, J. W. (1984). Determinants of student self-concept: Is it better to be a relatively large fish in a small pond even if you don't learn to swim as well? *Journal of Personality and Social Psychology 47*, 213–231.

Torrence, E. P. (1977). Discovery and nurturance of giftedness in the culturally different. *Council for Exceptional Children.* https://files.eric.ed.gov/fulltext/ED145621.pdf

OUTING

Learning Objectives

- Understand potential risks and unintended consequences of technology apps with unknown underlying mechanisms for sharing data.
- Understand the implications of using software that can detect private characteristics of students based on student responses in their writing.

Scenario Narrative

The Adelie School District recently bought new software to detect cheating and plagiarism. Teachers and administrators were trained to use the software and the analytics it produces. True to its intent, teachers were able to identify several cheating incidents.

Mr. Cappy was examining the output from one set of analyses and noticed that a student, Izzy, short for Isadore, used pronouns that were not for his gender. Instead of using he/him/his, Izzy used she/her/hers. The document was signed Isabel rather than Izzy. The pronouns were highlighted in the analytics as a potential problem. Mr. Cappy reported this to the principal, Mr. Woody, who then called Izzy's parents to discuss the matter. The parents were not aware of the situation and immediately confronted Izzy. The result was that the software had outed Izzy before the student was ready to discuss gender identity with their parents.

Discussion Questions

1. If you were Mr. Cappy, what would you have done with the information?
2. Should Mr. Cappy and the school administrators have access to the analytics?
3. What should Mr. Woody do?

Extending Activities

- Discuss the intended and unintended consequences, and the potential harms of using the analytics.
- Discuss the pros and cons of the use of detection software.
- Discuss what kinds of actions the educators should have taken in this situation.
- Consider whether the district should continue to use the software and the implications of doing so.

From the Evidence Vault

Ettinghoff, E. (2014). Outed at school: Student privacy rights and preventing unwanted disclosures of sexual orientation. *Loyola of Los Angeles Law Review, 47*(2), 1–42.

In the News

Baker, K. J. M. (2023, January 22). When students change gender identify and parents don't know. *New York Times*. https://www.nytimes.com/2023/01/22/us/gender-identity-students-parents.html?smid=nytcore-ios-share&referringSource=articleShare

Caraballo, A. (2022, February). Remote learning accidentally introduced a new danger for LGBTQ students. *Slate*. https://slate.com/technology/2022/02/remote-learning-danger-lgbtq-students.html

Teaching Notes

This scenario exposes several interesting issues. First, school districts should be made aware of the unintended consequences and potential misuses and harms that can ensue from data being pulled for purposes other than those intended, even if the intentions are reasonable. Identifying possible cheating would be based on specific algorithms. Higher education has used such detection programs for years. However, using these programs for analyses that could lead to potential harm to students or the release of confidential information is problematic. Vendors have been known to sell personally identifiable information. The vendor could claim that such analytics are used to protect the student from possible bullying as in the *Slate* article noted above. It seems more likely that the intention is more about uncovering highly personal information about students based on their writing. Certainly, if the program detects the potential for self-harm, suicide, bullying, or other such problematic behavior, then, as mandated reporters, the educators must act. But educators must be mindful of the fine line between confidential information and potential harm.

Ethics

Ethical issues abound in this scenario that relate to unintended consequences and potential harm. Do the educators have the right to "out" Izzy? Do they have the right to discuss their suspicions with Izzy's parents? Should the educators speak to Izzy with sensitivity and openness? What are the right courses of action based on such personal information? Should the district use the software for purposes other than to detect cheating, given the potential for uncovering personal information that students may share in their writing? How does the district balance detection of harmful information versus with something like revealing gender identity? Educators are obligated to protect the privacy and confidentiality of students.

This issue goes beyond detection through technology to conversations as well. In 2022, legislators in Arizona proposed a bill that would require teachers to "out" LGBTQA students (Macdonald-Evoy, 2022). The premise was that government employees, including educators, cannot withhold information about students' gender identity. Educators, therefore, would be required to report whether students had confided in them about being gay or transexual. Under the guise of "transparency," educators could face discipline or lawsuits if they failed to comply. Where are the boundaries for sharing information garnered from the analytics in the technology or even innocent conversations between a student and a teacher versus protecting that information, with the consideration of potential harms? What if educators could face charges for failing to report a conversation with a student? Students would no longer feel safe having a confidential conversation with a trusting educator, and educators would be torn for fear of punishment. Educators must consider the entire context in which the information was obtained and the appropriate uses. For example, what if Izzy's parents were anti-LGBTQA and rejected the emerging identity? In the case of "outing" via the technology platform, the district would have endangered the student by sharing the personal revelations. Obviously, major ethical ramifications underlie this scenario.

References and Resources

Office of Civil Rights. (n.d.). *Resources for LGBTQI+ students.* https://www2.ed.gov/about/offices/list/ocr/lgbt.html

ADOPTION

Learning Objectives

- Gain an appreciation for examining data beyond test scores.
- Gain an appreciation for looking at diverse data sources, especially health, socio-emotional well-being, and beyond.
- Understand the need to examine contextual variables and the whole child.

Scenario Narrative

Jemma is a student at Watson Middle School. She has always been a good student and diligent in her work. Jemma was adopted at 18 months from a foreign country. She just celebrated her 13th birthday. Then something of unknown origin happened, and Jemma began acting out. She refused to go to school. She simply would stay in her room with her pets. Her mother, Mrs. Skylar, tried repeatedly to get Jemma to go to school without success. If she got Jemma into the car and they drove to school, Jemma would refuse to get out of the car. Mrs. Skylar contacted administrators at Watson as well as Jemma's homeroom teacher, Mr. Fritz, to arrange a homeschooling option whereby the teachers would send her Jemma's assignments to be completed at home.

Mrs. Skylar requested a meeting with Mr. Fritz as well as the principal, Mr. Winchester, to seek information about the potential that Jemma might have been bullied. Were students making fun of her? Was there an incident of bullying? Were kids mocking her because she was adopted? Could there be a medical explanation? None of these explanations seemed to pertain. She also asked about their observations concerning Jemma's behavior, performance, and anything else that might lend insights into why she suddenly refused to go to school. Mrs. Skylar questioned whether Jemma had sought assistance from an educator, a counselor, confided in the school nurse, or someone else. Were there indications or explanations for the changed behavior? Mrs. Skylar also sought help from their family physician.

As Mrs. Skylar continued to seek explanations, Mr. Fritz and Mr. Winchester developed a work-around plan for temporary homeschooling while the issue got sorted out. Jemma maintained decent grades but still refused to attend school. Looking at just her academic performance, one would think everything was all right, but it wasn't.

Discussion Questions

1. What do you think Mr. Winchester should do?
2. What do you think Mr. Fritz should do?
3. What responsibility might the school nurse or the guidance counselor have?
4. What course of action should Mrs. Skylar take?

Extending Activities

- Discuss possible explanations for Jemma's sudden resistance to school.
- Discuss what should be done if it is found that Jemma had been bullied.
- Discuss what should be done if Jemma has a medical issue. Who has the right to know about that condition?
- Overall, what position should educators take concerning Jemma refusing to come to school?
- Discuss the fact that Jemma continues to perform academically but still resists entering the school building.
- Discuss which data points might be used to help understand Jemma's situation.

From the Evidence Vault

Torrens Armstrong, A. M. (2011). Frequent fliers, school phobias, and the sick student: School health personnel's perceptions of students who refuse school. *Journal of School Health, 81*(9).

In the News

Chang, E. (2022, September). What to do, and not do, when your child won't go to school. *Washington Post*. https://www.washingtonpost.com/parenting/2022/09/22/school-avoidance-refusal-tips/

Teaching Notes

This scenario requires educators to consider the whole child. If educators were to look solely at student performance metrics, Jemma would appear to be okay. But she clearly is not. Something happened to cause this change in behavior, either at school or elsewhere. Even if the cause occurred elsewhere, it is still impacting the educational process. The educators, working in collaboration with Mrs. Skylar, rightly sought a temporary fix until an explanation or a more permanent solution could be found. But is isolating Jemma through homeschooling the right fix? Does it depend on the explanation, for example, if Jemma were being bullied? What if the explanation has medical roots, such as mental illness, anxiety, hormonal imbalance, or something else? What if the explanation relates to having been adopted, a fact that cannot be changed? The educators must consider the boundaries and work with Mrs. Skylar to develop not just a short-term fix but also a long-term plan.

Ethics

Because this scenario requires multiple individuals and multiple data sources, there must be a collaborative approach, one sufficiently sensitive to Mrs. Skylar and Jemma's needs. This may mean limiting the scope of the inquiry to those directly involved and knowledgeable. It may mean communicating with Jemma's medical professionals to seek a potential solution but with the proper protection of her privacy. Data should be shared on a need-to-know basis, especially if the data crosses FERPA or HIIPA boundaries. Caution and sensitivity must be used. The objective is to restore Jemma's functioning, depending on the root cause.

One of the biggest challenges in this scenario is the triangulation of data to help understand Jemma's situation. There also may be data privacy barriers. That said, if educators looked only at performance data, Jemma would be doing fine. But the broader examination of diverse data leads to a very different picture. It is essential for the professionals to bring together their sources of data to inform the situation. By taking a narrow view, the potential is for harmful consequences.

References and Resources

Busman, R. (2022). How to recognize what's called "school refusal" and how to get kids back in class. *Child Mind Institute.* https://childmind.org/article/when-kids-refuse-to-go-to-school/

Wimmer, M. (2008). What kids refuse to go to school . . . and what schools can do about it. *Education Digest, 74*(3), 32–37. tps://www.proquest.com/openview/f133d28139bd35da9eada32052c27b9b/1.pdf?pq-origsite=gscholar&cbl=25066

Wimmer, M. (2010). School refusal: Information for educators. *National Association of School Psychologists.* https://www.woodstown.org/cms/lib4/NJ01001783/Centricity/Domain/374/School_Refusal_Information_for_Educators-2.pdf

CONFIRMATION BIAS

Learning Objectives

- Learn about the implications of stereotypes, attributions, and confirmation bias that can lead to harmful consequences for groups of students and individual students.
- Learn about deficit thinking.

Introductory Comment

This scenario is intended to push the envelope about the stereotypic ways people may think about certain demographic groups. No offense is intended. The scenario seeks to force users to think about how unconscious bias, stereotypes, confirmation bias, and attributions are used and can create potential harm.

Scenario Narrative

Ms. Sally is the math department chair at Boss High School. Boss has a high percentage of lower- to middle-income, immigrant students from Southeast Asia. The students are typically second generation, but there are also some first-generation students. These students come from many different countries and cultures. For some students, language is a barrier, whereas other students are more fluent. Language, however, is a barrier at home, as many of the students' parents speak only their native language.

Ms. Sally has made it clear to her department that they are to hold high expectations for all students but also provide accommodations where needed to compensate for language barriers and other possible challenges. In departmental meetings, some teachers assume that because the students are of Asian origin, they have a natural proclivity toward STEM disciplines. They make biased assumptions that all Asians are similar, regardless of their cultural backgrounds. Other teachers have discussed how language is a barrier, even for second-generation students. The teachers do not intend to sound biased; they are simply making comments based on their observations.

Benchmark assessments are given to the freshmen and sophomores. The results run the full continuum. Discussion among the teachers is telling. Some teachers blame the students who struggled because of their language challenges; others blamed lack of effort or even home environment for not supporting student learning. Their discussions clearly focus on student deficits. Some teachers fully expected most student to pass because of their cultural backgrounds, assuming that Asian students are good at math. Not one teacher discusses the results in terms of their own instructional strategies, the alignment of the test to their curriculum, or activities that are under their control. The blame for the results is firmly grounded in student characteristics.

Discussion Questions

1. How did stereotypes and confirmation bias manifest in the departmental discussions?
2. As the department chair, how should Ms. Sally redirect the discussion?

Extending Activities

- Discuss how deficit thinking can negatively permeate teachers' thinking and the implications for classroom practice.
- Discuss how an asset model might be established more readily.
- Discuss how confirmation bias and attribution theory play out in this scenario.

From the Evidence Vault

Bertrand, M., & Marsh, J. A. (2015). Teachers' sensemaking of data and implications for equity. *American Educational Research Journal, 52*(5), 861–893.

Bertrand, M., & Marsh, J. A. (2021, May). How data-driven reform can drive deficit thinking. *PDK, 102*(8), 35–39.

Nickerson, R. S. (1998). Confirmation bias: A ubiquitous phenomenon in many guises. *Review of General Psychology, 2*(2), 175–220.

In the News

Plata, G. S. (2019, July). Not all Asian Americans are the same. So why do school data treat us that way. *Education Week*. https://www.edweek.org/leadership/opinion-not-all-asian-americans-are-the-same-so-why-do-school-data-treat-us-that-way/2019/07

Toppa, S. (2021, April). Students labeled "Asian" are not a monolith. Why are schools treating them that way? *TFA*. https://www.teachforamerica.org/one-day/policy-and-advocacy/students-labeled-asian-are-not-a-monolith-why-are-schools-treating-them

Teaching Notes

This scenario deals with several fundamental concepts about how individuals make assumptions that are often unfounded and how they manifest in actions. First, making assumptions about a particular demographic group is wrong, such as the stereotype that all Asians are good at STEM. Second, Asians are diverse. There are many cultures and many differences, so it is inappropriate to make such broad categorizations. Thus, the scenario speaks to the issue of using stereotypes and broad generalizations. Third, the scenario deals with the use of a deficit model (i.e., that the students lack certain skills or perform poorly because of student characteristics). Fourth, the scenario deals with confirmation bias: the teachers assume something to be true, and the results play out for those Asian students who performed well on the benchmarks. Finally, the scenario touches on the use of attributions: blaming students for poor performance based on their characteristics as opposed to examining how instruction might be modified or the extent to which characteristics of the test align with the curriculum. Each of these topics is relevant in this scenario.

Ethics

Using a deficit model, engaging in confirmation bias, and using stereotypes to categorize students are all problematic practices. Teachers should examine how their instruction, the curricula, and the means of assessment relate to student performance, rather than blaming the students' nonmalleable characteristics for the failures. Making broad generalizations is problematic—all X should succeed or fail. Every student is an individual who brings to the classroom this own assets, interests, cultures, contexts, and home circumstances. It is important for educators to adopt an asset mind-set to help all students succeed.

References and Resources

Paik, S. J., Rabman, Z., et al. (2017). Diverse Asian American families and communicates: Culture, structure, and education (Part 1: Why they differ). *School Community Journal, 27*(2), 35–66.

JOCKS

Learning Objectives

- Learn about preconceived notions about specific groups of students.
- Understand issues about confirmation bias.

Introductory Comment

This is one of the scenarios written with the specific intent to address explicit stereotypes. The purpose is not to offend but, rather, to highlight the inappropriateness of stereotypes and their potential harm.

Scenario Narrative

Winston High School is known for its athletics program. The school has a full range of sports, and both males and females participate to the fullest extent. Mocha is the star quarterback.

Maximilian is an outstanding tennis player. Ava is a soccer goalie. Zoey is a golfer. Remi is a baseball player. Hazel is a swimmer. Mr. Digit is a new teacher who came from another school that let its athletes slip by academically, giving them a reputation for being "dumb jocks," to use a pejorative term. In the first few weeks of class, Mr. Digit makes assumptions about the extent to which the student-athletes can grasp concepts such as acceleration and velocity in his physics class. He is frankly amazed that athletes would even be enrolled in an advanced class such as physics. Mr. Digit starts his classes, and the students seem really bored. He is teaching down to them on topics they already seem to know, so the students are not especially engaged.

In an early assignment, Mr. Digit asks the student to write about how physics concepts are relevant in their everyday life. He is blown away by some of the responses. Mocha, the football player, describes how he understands the rotation of the football, the necessary arc of a pass, and the speed with which the ball is thrown to reach a receiver, with specific timing and accuracy. Maximilian, the tennis player, describes how the various spins of the tennis ball relate to rotation, racquet acceleration, and placement in the court. Ava, the goalie, describes how she must time her saves, based on the arc, speed, angle, and trajectory of a kick. Zoey writes about how she accelerates different golf clubs, based on the lie of the ball, the distance to the pin, and other characteristics to create loft and distance. Remi describes how he gauges the location of the baseball after it leaves the bat, based on height, trajectory, and speed. Hazel writes about the arc and depth of her dive off the starting blocks and how she maximizes drag while in the lane and on her flip turn. Mr. Digit has significantly underestimated these students and needs to adjust his expectations and instructional strategies.

Discussion Questions

1. Why do you think Mr. Digit underestimated the student athletes?
2. What do you think about stereotyping students based on certain characteristics?

Extending Activities

- Discuss the concept of stereotyping and how it can impact teachers' perceptions of and strategies toward different groups of students.
- Discuss how the student athletes applied knowledge of physics to their sports, dispelling the notion that athletes are not smart.

From the Evidence Vault

Longo, G. (2015). *Scoring a goal about the "Dumb Jock" stereotype.* https://scholarsarchive.jwu.edu/cgi/viewcontent.cgi?article=1029&context=ac_symposium

Steele, C. M., & Aronson, J. (1998). Stereotype threat and the test performance of academically successful African Americans. In C. Jencks & M. Phillips (Eds.), *The Black–White Test Score Gap* (pp. 401–427). Brookings Institution Press.

In the News

Barrett, J. (2017, March). The stereotype of athletes: Dumb jock syndrome. *The Equinox.* https://kscequinox.com/2017/03/the-stereotype-of-athletes-dumb-jock-syndrome/

Teaching Notes

Mr. Digit approached his class with preconceived ideas that athletes were not necessarily strong students, particularly in an advanced course such as physics. Many types of stereotypes cause teachers to have inaccurate perspectives about certain groups of students. Athletes are one. The assumption is that they simply get a pass on challenging academic courses so they can play their sport. This is just wrong. Just because an athlete struggles in a course does not mean that he or she cannot learn. Fundamental concepts in many sports are part of science and math, for example. Football players must learn a complex playbook. They remember patterns. They understand trajectory, angles, and more. Good tennis players easily recognize angles, different spins, trajectories, speed, ball rotation, and patterns that enable them to be in the right place on court and prepared to hit another ball. An effective teaching strategy is to tap into athletes' and other students' interests. Mr. Digit used a good instructional strategy to see how students used their experiences, in this case in sports, to provide evidence of their understanding of the physics concepts and their application to the various sports.

Ethics

Making assumptions about what students can and cannot learn based on various characteristics is a bad practice. A large research literature about confirmation bias, stereotype threat, and attribution is relevant here. Teachers should not make assumptions about their students. Mr. Digit tapped students' interests and backgrounds as a good instructional strategy discussed in the culturally responsive teaching literature.

References and Resources

Nickerson, R. S. (1998). Confirmation bias: A ubiquitous phenomenon in many guises. *Review of General Psychology, 2*(2), 175–220.

Wretman, C. (2017). School sports participation and academic achievement in middle and high school. *Journal of the Society for Social Work and Research, 8*(3), 1–22. https://www.journals.uchicago.edu/doi/10.1086/693117

SIBLING HISTORY

Learning Objectives

- Learn that each student is an individual—that is, familial history may be informative, but each child is unique.
- Learn to consider the unique factors for each student.
- Understand that preconceived notions about a student, based on past history with siblings, is not good practice.

Scenario Narrative

Coco is a high-school freshman who was assigned to the same teacher her sister Paisley had a few years previously. Apparently, Paisley garnered quite a reputation. Upon entering her first English class with Ms. Maeve, the teacher exclaims, "Oh, so you are Paisley's sister! I expect from you the same high standard of performance."

Coco is unsure how to react and sort of shrugs off the comment. However, comments keep coming over several weeks. They reflect that Paisley was an outstanding student and that Coco is expected to live up to the family history. Coco feels pressured. She is a good student, but should she be expected to live up to her sister in everything she does? Coco mentions the issue to her parents, but at school she tries to ignore the comments. Ms. Maeve seems oblivious to the comparisons, as she tends to make similar comparisons with other students. It is a small community, and everyone knows everyone else, so the comparisons of siblings seem like a natural thing to do. Especially when the older sibling is a good student, Ms. Maeve believes this to be a motivating strategy. The problem for Coco is that she is constantly being compared to Paisley, who set a high bar in school and other activities, and she is getting tired of this treatment. At the first parent-teacher conference, Ms. Maeve makes some similar comparisons to Coco's parents.

Discussion Questions

1. How should Coco have handled the situation?
2. Do you think Ms. Maeve did anything wrong? Why or why not?
3. Should Coco's parents call out Ms. Maeve for her comments?

Extending Activities

- Discuss why it is a good or bad idea to make comparisons among siblings.
- Describe what sort of data points Ms. Maeve should use to evaluate Coco's performance and behavior.
- Discuss more broadly the practice of making comparisons across students.
- Extend this scenario. Would your reactions differ in any way if Paisley had been a poor student or had had behavioral issues?
- Discuss how Coco's parents should react in the parent-teacher conference.

From the Evidence Vault

Richey L. S., & Ysseldyke, J. E. (2016). Teachers' expectations for the younger siblings of learning disabled students. *Journal of Learning Disabilities, 16*(10).

In the News

Krauss, A. (2018, November). Teachers comparing siblings is not ideal for the student. *The Lariat*. http://www.thelariatonline.com/teachers-comparing-siblings-is-not-ideal-for-the-student/

Teaching Notes

Every student deserves to be treated as an individual without preconceived notions based on siblings or other students. Family history can provide invaluable information. However, even within a family, circumstances can change over time, impacting subsequent students. For example, there could be familial disruptions such as a divorce, separation, or financial issues. Family context is one of many data points to which a teacher can turn to understand a student. Preconceived notions or beliefs ultimately can lead to unconscious bias or other negative actions. Such beliefs can lead to unreasonable expectations, either too high or too low.

What would happen if a teacher had twins in the same class? Would the teacher treat the twins identically or as individuals? Users should think back to their own personal histories and recall whether they were compared to their siblings and, if so, how they felt.

Ethics

Comparing students can be a risky endeavor as each student is an individual and brings unique characteristics to the classroom. Even if the intention is positive, the interpretation of such comparative statements may create undue harm and unintended consequences. And now with many merged families, educators should not make assumptions about familiar relationships and base remarks on those assumptions. The collection of data points for each individual student is a safer, more practical course of action.

The use of information about a sibling or any other student can lead to preconceived notions about a given student. It can lead to confirmation bias. Even using home circumstances that a teacher would know from an older sibling may no longer be accurate as context can change over time. Obtaining a full scope of data in such instances would mean being careful to ascertain whether older information is still correct and updating other information as appropriate.

References and Resources

Rosenthal, R., & Jacobson, L. (1968). *Pygmalion in the Classroom*. Holt, Rinehart, & Winston.

FACIAL RECOGNITION

Learning Objectives

- Understand that some technologies may be unable to detect differences in accents or speech patterns for different groups of students.
- Understand that facial recognition software may inherently be unable to detect patterns equally across races and ethnicities.

Scenario Narrative

The Bruno School District has put into place facial recognition procedures for school IDs for students and staff. The district made these decisions expecting that the schools will be safer to have facial recognition rather than ID cards that can be falsified more readily. Mr. Gucci is the vice principal of one of Bruno's schools. He has been getting a barrage of reports from teachers that many students are late for class, especially first period. Reports from the teachers indicate that many of the tardy students are students of color. More and more students are being delayed by the recognition technology, which maintains that the students are not who they say they are and do not belong in the school. Mr. Gucci does not want to make any assumptions about the reasons for their trend, but he begins to investigate.

Discussion Questions

1. What explanations might there be for the students being delayed?
2. What do you think Mr. Gucci and the district should do?

Extending Activities

- Discuss whether you think facial recognition should be used and whether it is a better option than ID cards or other techniques.
- Discuss what you think of Bruno's explanation that the recognition technology would make the schools safer.

From the Evidence Vault

Andrejevic, M., & Selwyn, N. (2018). Facial recognition technology in schools: Critical questions and concerns. *Learning, Media and Technology, 45*(2), 115–128.

In the News

Alba, D. (2020, February). Facial recognition moves into a new front: Schools. *New York Times*. https://www.nytimes.com/2020/02/06/business/facial-recognition-schools.html

Najibi, A. (2020, October). *Racial discrimination in face recognition technology.* https://sitn.hms.harvard.edu/flash/2020/racial-discrimination-in-face-recognition-technology/

Teaching Notes

Districts should be mindful about adopting technologies that may have the potential for bias and discrimination based on the underlying algorithms of the software. This could include facial recognition, voice recognition, or other sorts of technologies that rely on determinations about voice patterns, speaking patterns, appearance, and more. In the case of Bruno, the fact that the facial recognition system is failing to recognize students of color is a discriminatory practice. The data being used are fraught with problems, based on the underlying algorithms of the technology. The teachers are right to bring the perceived trend to the attention of building and district leadership as the technologies are inaccurately highlighting subgroups of students who should not be admitted to the building.

Ethics

The biggest concern about the use of technologies such as facial or voice recognition is whether the technologies can recognize all individuals without possible bias. In the past, the technologies have been shown to be less sensitive when trying to discern the facial patterns of individuals of color. Similarly, voice recognition has been problematic for voices that are non-native speakers, speakers with accents, or those with regional or ethnic voice dialects. If the technologies are in any way biased and cannot equally perform the detection functions, then the data that ensue are troublesome, and the district should consider alternative solutions. For teachers using voice recognition on computers for instructional purposes, such embedded bias can be extremely problematic in implementing appropriate instructional practices.

References and Resources

Orchison, M. (2021, November). *The problem with facial recognition in schools.* https://www.9ine.com/newsblog/the-problem-with-facial-recognition-in-schools

Chapter 5

The Scenarios Continued

Below are the remaining 21 scenarios. Again, they are presented in no specific order.

Holiday Awareness
Religious Expression
Snacks
Language Is Beautiful
Dress Code
Referrals
Mental Health
Body Shaming and Bullying
Hug Therapy
Self-Harm or Abuse
Overlooking Socio-Emotional Well-Being
Mouthing While Singing
Silence
Attendance and Chronic Absences
Gaming the System
Manipulating Performance
To Test or Not to Test
Nutrition Activity
Physical Activity
Size Matters

HOLIDAY AWARENESS

Learning Objectives
- Understand that different religions have different holiday observances than those noted on the national holiday calendar. Some major holidays may be excluded from school holiday calendars.
- Recognize the legitimacy of those observances and the religious diversity among students and teachers.
- Understand the importance of being respectful of different religions' observances, trying not to schedule major events (e.g., tests, athletics events, etc.) on those holidays.

Scenario Narrative

Pearl is a student at Summer High School in a small regional district in a rural state. The student population is not diverse. Pearl happens to be Jewish, the only one in the school. The Jewish holidays are approaching. Pearl takes a day off for Rosh Hashanah and another for Yom Kippur. Following the holidays, the school sends an email to Pearl's parents saying that her explanation for the absence is unacceptable. They also discovered that school pictures were scheduled during the holidays, so Pearl missed that opportunity. Pearl's parents, the Lokis, are angry at the insensitivity on the part of the district. Pearl's parents make an appointment with the principal, Mr. Lake. They hope to make Mr. Lake and the district aware of the need to be inclusive of all religions, not just mainstream Christian ones.

Discussion Questions

1. What position should Mr. Lake take?
2. Do the two issues (the scheduling of the school pictures and the absence policy) have similar footing?
3. What rights do Pearl's parents have?

Extending Activities

- Discuss what would have happened had the holidays been Good Friday, Ramadan, or other major holidays for other religions.
- Discuss the perspective of the district if such actions have also happened to Muslim students during Ramadan.
- Discuss whether a religious holiday is an appropriate basis for an excused absence.
- Discuss what should happen to future school schedules.
- Discuss how the school or district might become more aware of religious differences and the impact on students, teachers, and the community.

From the Evidence Vault

Marshall, J. M. (2016, June). Religion and education: Walking the line in public schools. *PDK, 85*(3). https://doi.org/10.1177/003172170308500315

Whitaker, C. R., Salend, S., & Elhoweris, H. (2009). Religious diversity in schools: Addressing issues. *Intervention in School and Clinic, 4*(5), 314–319. https://doi.org/10.1177/1053451208330892

In the News

Blumofe, N. (2022, October). When curriculum standards and religion collide, students and faith traditions lose. *USA Today*. https://www.usatoday.com/story/opinion/voices/2022/10/15/school-boards-politicizing-religion-cirriculum-students-disservice/8199156001/

Stauber, E. (2018, October). Williamson schools exam policy penalizes kids who observe religious holidays, some say. *The Tennessean*. https://www.tennessean.com/story/news/local/williamson/2018/10/05/williamson-schools-religious-holidays-exam-exemption/1491734002/

Teaching Notes

Given the increasing diversity of student populations, there is a pressing need for educators to understand the religious holidays that may impact district schedules. This involves excusing groups of students for their own holidays, limiting celebrations that may offend some students, examining food services policies, and more. These practices and the awareness may become challenging, given the many backgrounds students present. At the very least, educators must become aware of holidays and practices that prevent some students from attending or participating in certain activities. For example, educators should be aware of dietary restrictions for Muslim and Jewish students. Convening a birthday party or a holiday celebration would be offensive to students who are Jehovah's Witnesses. Muslim students fast during Ramadan. Educators must be aware of and exhibit sensitivity to student needs and differences. Some may think this is a lot to ask of educators, but it speaks to the need for sensitivity to diversity.

Ethics

Student religion is not typically an educational data point. It is a demographic data point. It is valued information for educators as it helps to understand home context, beliefs, and other behavior. In typical practice, students' religious affiliations should not impact classroom practices. It does, however, help to provide valuable personal and home context information. Take, for example, an assignment in home economics to make ham, bacon, or pork would be problematic for observant Muslims and Jews. Hindu students would avoid beef. Educators must be aware of religious observances that could impact the schedule. Holding an event on Chinese or Vietnamese New Year, Yom Kippur, Good Friday, Ramadan, or other important dates is wrong and insensitive. Jehovah's Witnesses are not allowed to participate in parties or celebrations and should not be penalized for their lack of participation in, for example, a Christmas concert. Accommodations must be made based on knowledge about students' backgrounds and affiliations. Therefore, having the data about religious affiliation can help educators to address

- a student's refusal to eat or prepare certain foods,
- a student who brings a Bible to school as her favorite book,
- an absence from school for holiday observance,
- a student who refuses to sing the national anthem or salute the flag,
- a student wearing a head scarf or yarmulke, and
- a student who needs to pray at specific times of the day.

References and Resources

Lupu, I. C., Masci, D., & Tuttle, R. W. (n.d.). Religion in the public schools. *Pew Research Center*. https://www.pewresearch.org/religion/2019/10/03/religion-in-the-public-schools-2019-update/#prayer-and-the-pledge

RELIGIOUS EXPRESSION

Learning Objectives

- Consider how educators balance religious freedom and academic practice and policies.
- Consider how different religions may express their religion in school.

Scenario Narrative

Maya Middle School has recently had an influx of new students after their private schools closed. These sixth-grade students come from different religious backgrounds, and certain behaviors and beliefs reflect those backgrounds. Katie is a Jehovah's Witness who is unable to engage in celebrations, parties, or holidays. She cannot take part in certain activities or assignments that violate her religion, such as singing in a Christmas event. Freya is a Muslim student who has dietary limitations and wears a head scarf. Norman is an observant Jew who has never been to school with girls. He also has dietary restrictions.

Administrators and teachers at Maya are seeking strategies to accommodate the needs of the new students so that they do not infringe on their religious practices. It is difficult. Teachers must consider how to avoid curriculum materials that might violate Katie's practices. They must protect Freya's need for modesty, for example, in physical education. They also must consider food restrictions for both Freya and Norman in the cafeteria and elsewhere. They must consider whether it is reasonable to continue to isolate Norman from girls in seating plans and other activities. Each religion brings to the school different restrictions, holidays, and practices.

Discussion Questions

1. Should the educators at Maya be expected to review policies to accommodate all the needs of these new students?
2. How might the educators effectively accommodate the students?

Extending Activities

- Discuss the balance of religious freedom that may or may not be part of school policy.
- Discuss just how far educators must go to accommodate all religious practices.
- Discuss how some accommodations might be made in classroom management, while others may be related to curricula.

From the Evidence Vault

Frid, C., & Alexander, S. L. (2022). Accommodating religious practice at an elementary school: A case study. *Journal of Cases in Educational Leadership, 25*(3), 284–291.

In the News

Blumofe, N. (2022, October). When curriculum standards and religion collide, students and faith traditions lose. *USA Today.* https://www.usatoday.com/story/opinion/voices/2022/10/15/school-boards-politicizing-religion-cirriculum-students-disservice/8199156001/

Goldstein, D. (2022, April). Florida rejects math textbooks, citing "prohibited topics." *New York Times.* https://www.nytimes.com/2022/04/18/us/florida-math-textbooks-critical-race-theory.html

Patel, V. (2023, January). After lecturer sues, Hamline University walks back its "Islamophobic" comments. *New York Times.* https://www.nytimes.com/2023/01/17/us/hamline-lawsuit-prophet-muhammad-religion.html

Patel, V. (2023, January). A lecturer showed a painting of the Prophet Muhammad. She lost her job. *New York Times.* https://www.nytimes.com/2023/01/08/us/hamline-university-islam-prophet-muhammad.html

Shapiro, E., & Rosenthal, B. M. (2022, September). In Hasidic enclaves, failing private schools flush with public money. *New York Times.* https://www.nytimes.com/2022/09/11/nyregion/hasidic-yeshivas-schools-new-york.html

Teaching Notes

Schools must do their best to respond to and be sensitive to students' backgrounds. But it requires a delicate balance. Much has been written in the public media about the expression of religious freedom in society (i.e., the acceptance of Muslim females wearing head coverings or Jewish males wearing yarmulkes). Take, for example, (a) a strictly religious Jewish man who refuses to sit next to a woman on a plane; (b) public funds being expended to yeshivas where the students get limited or no formal education in reading, math, and other foundational subjects and exclude females; (c) Muslim students who have been harassed for wearing head coverings; (d) students who refuse to be vaccinated on the basis of religious freedom; or (e) religious groups objecting to various parts of curricula. There are many incidents of cultural insensitivity. In part, it is why some religious groups choose to educate their own children, isolating them from the mainstream and broader curricula. Yet, recent public media have expressed concern that such isolated educational experiences further marginalize students by not adequately preparing them with the basic skills for functioning in society. This has been the case with yeshivas that focus on religious studies to the exclusion of foundational content areas (Shapiro & Rosenthal, 2022).

Ethics

Using cultural sensitivity is essential, particularly in understanding how students' backgrounds may influence their behavior. What may be acceptable in school policy may be unacceptable in their practices and vice versa. Issues arise when the two sets of principles are at odds. For example, an art history instructor at a college prepared students for a discussion about a piece of art about which the Muslim students objected. Despite an extensive discussion about the specific piece of art to prepare students, the Muslim students complained, and the instructor was fired, but later reinstated (Patel, 2023).

How do schools balance curricular issues where certain content may be objectionable to specific groups of students? What are the appropriate accommodations? How far should or must schools go to modify their curricula for some students? In the art history example, the piece of art was considered a masterpiece by scholars, so does this work remain in the curricula with adequate preparation and discussion or is it excised because it is objectionable to some students? Should certain books be removed from the curricula? Should certain math problems be removed? This has become a divisive issue in certain regions of the country.

References and Resources

Lupu, I. C., Masci, D., & Tuttle, R. W. (n.d.). Religion in the public schools. *Pew Research Center.* https://www.pewresearch.org/religion/2019/10/03/religion-in-the-public-schools-2019-update/#prayer-and-the-pledge

SNACKS

Learning Objectives

- Recognize that students may have different requirements around food, whether an allergy or medical issue, a religious requirement, or simply a preference.
- Understand the need to be sensitive and not make assumptions about snacks in terms of whether students can afford to bring their own food.

Scenario Narrative

Mr. Henry is a first-grade teacher at Poppy, a diverse school district. He has students from different religions. He has students who come from impoverished homes; some are unhoused or live in homeless shelters. Some students, as he suspects, may have medical issues. Every day, Mr. Henry convenes a snack time where students can relax without any academics and have social interaction. The district provides snacks for students who cannot afford them. Other students bring their own snacks. It is time out of the day where they do not have to worry about learning activities. And for some, it is another opportunity for them to be provided much-needed food. The food that the district provides can be a challenge due to religious restrictions, medical conditions, or even student food preferences.

During snack time, Mr. Henry tries to engage students in broad conversation to elicit information about things they like to do, hobbies, interests, or whatever is on their mind. Mr. Henry tries to make snack time an inclusive activity. But at times he observes certain students not partaking or participating. He tries to determine the sources of the reluctance. It could be that the students are uncomfortable talking about certain topics. It could be that they have a medical issue. It could be that they feel uncomfortable being categorized for receiving food rather than bringing their own. Mr. Henry is really trying to meet the needs of all his students and be sensitive.

Discussion Questions

1. What do you think about Mr. Henry's practices and strategies?
2. How might Mr. Henry learn more about the students?

Extending Activities

- Discuss how educators can meet the needs of diverse students while not negatively impacting them in any way.
- Discuss how educators can help students who may have impediments, such as financial resources, in a situation like this scenario.

From the Evidence Vault

Castellari, E., & Berning, J. P. (2016, November). Can providing a morning healthy snack help to reduce hunger during school time? Experimental evidence from an elementary school in Connecticut. *Appetite, 106*, 70–77. doi: 10.1016/j.appet.2016.02.157.

In the News

Renee, J. (2018, November). What are the benefits of children eating snacks during school? *SFGATE*. https://healthyeating.sfgate.com/benefits-children-eating-snacks-during-school-4999.html

Teaching Notes

Students have food preferences and dislikes. Some students have medical conditions that prevent them from eating certain foods. Some students have religious restrictions about food. Some students cannot afford their own food. Educators must be sensitive to and considerate of these differences for events such as snack time. Understanding the needs may require discussions with counselors, school nurses, parents, and students. Teachers should be alert when a student withdraws and does not participate. They should try to understand the root cause and seek solutions.

Ethics

A whole child approach is necessary to understand the context of the students and determine the explanations for participation or lack of participation in an activity such as snack time. Are teachers aware of food allergies or other medical conditions (e.g., gluten free, peanut allergy)? That would be a form of data. Are teachers aware of a religious restriction? For example, observant Muslim, Jewish, and Hindu students are provided with a food product that is restricted by their religion. Are teachers aware that certain students may not have the resources to bring their own food? All of these are critical data points to which teachers should and must be sensitive.

References and Resources

Many school districts and state departments of education provide guidelines and policies for what are acceptable snacks. Search for your locale to obtain the appropriate information.

LANGUAGE IS BEAUTIFUL

Learning Objectives

- Recognize that different cultures have different and acceptable ways of speaking.
- Acknowledge that different accents, languages, dialects, and patterns of speech are acceptable forms of communication.

Scenario Narrative

The Winslow School District is in the South. Many accents can be heard across the district. There are Southern accents. There are also many newly arrived immigrant students, so it is not just accents but also different languages and dialects from their native countries. There are also transplants from other parts of the United States, all with regional dialects, ways of speaking, idioms, and vocabulary. The district truly is a melting pot. In addition, there are students who have speech impairments that impact their ability to communicate. These might include a lisp, a stutter, or something more severe such as an individual who has had to learn to speak with a hearing impairment.

Educators make every effort to be sensitive to speech differences. But sometimes they simply cannot understand their students and have an impulse to correct students who fail to use "proper English." The district uses interpreters and translators as needed. Some students even make fun of others who do not speak "right." For example, they mock a student who stutters to the point that the student no longer likes to speak aloud. They may make fun of a strong accent or a particular term that is unfamiliar but is a regionalism. The district tries to be inclusive and accepting but struggles to attain a balance—celebrating a student's roots and heritage while also trying to teach language arts.

Discussion Questions

1. Is there one acceptable way to deal with language arts?
2. Should a district focus only on what is considered "proper English"?

Extending Activities

- Discuss the issue of inclusivity around the diversity of language styles.
- Discuss what you think should be accepted language.
- Discuss what you think about the phrase "all language is beautiful."
- Discuss whether you think there are boundaries around acceptable language.

In the News

Blackley, A. (2019, April). It's not uncommon for schools to have dozens of home languages—and our classrooms need to reflect that. *We Are Teachers*. https://www.weareteachers.com/many-different-home-languages/

From the Evidence Vault

Huynh, T. (2022, February). Incorporating students' native languages to enhance their learning. *Edutopia*. https://www.edutopia.org/article/incorporating-students-native-languages-enhance-their-learning/

Teaching Notes

It is important in the whole child perspective to be accepting of and accommodating toward students' cultural backgrounds. The asset model would say that native language should be celebrated and seen as an asset students bring to the classroom. Educators must find ways to balance language arts teaching while capitalizing on the skills students bring to the classroom. It is inappropriate to mock a student's accent or language challenges.

Ethics

Discriminating against students because of language patterns in wrong. School districts that have many nonnative students with multiple languages and dialects may require translators. There may be students with hearing impairments that require interpreters. A school may be a melting pot of many accents, all acceptable as part of students' heritages and background. Questions remain about pushing students to subsume their native language. Using

CRDL stresses the need to understand the differences while accepting and supporting those differences.

References and Resources

Oliva-Olson, C., Espinoza L. M., Hayslip, W., & Magruder, E. S. (2019, December–January). Many languages, one classroom: Supporting children in superdiverse settings. *Teaching Young Children, 12*(2). https://www.naeyc.org/resources/pubs/tyc/dec2018/supporting-children-superdiverse-settings

DRESS CODE

Learning Objectives

- Recognize that cultural differences need to be considered when interpreting data and making decisions.
- Recognize that body shaming and other such behavior is unacceptable and can be perpetuated by school policies.

Scenario Narrative

The Jackson School serves a diverse population of students in an urban area. Jackson has established a strict dress code and is now considering a uniform policy to address competition among students, inappropriate dress, as well as clothing related to specific groups (e.g., political affiliations, gangs, etc.). The intent of the policy would be to equalize students and instill pride in themselves and their school beyond being defined by what they wear. Some students in the past have gone over the top with expensive designer clothing. Other students have made statements by wearing certain expensive athletic shoes, while other students have attempted to make questionable statements through T-shirts and other articles of clothing.

Currently, the dress code specifies no tight-fitting clothing, no super-baggy clothes, and nothing that shows flesh. The unstated objective for these policies is to minimize body shaming. If a uniform policy were to be adopted, it would make accommodations for different body types.

Clarice is a seventh-grade student who already has developed a mature body. Other students, like Oakley, are not nearly as developed. Students tend to stare at Clarice. She is proud of her development and sometimes makes this fact known in front of other students. At other times, she is self-conscious. Clarice has seen professional athletes who have similar body types. These athletes have received disparaging comments about their choice of clothing because the clothes have been too tight, too revealing, or simply unattractive in the eyes of other people.

Ms. Winnie is a physical education teacher at Jackson. She has seen middle-school girls with all sorts of body types, at different stages of maturation, and she tries to help all students attain a level of physical fitness and self-confidence. However, her view of what fitness looks like might differ from others. She never says anything directly to disparage different body types, but she clearly believes that slender is better than curvy. As a PE teacher, Ms. Winnie is well aware that middle-school students can be self-conscious and extremely concerned about their stage of development. It is a sensitive topic. She also recognizes that acceptable body images may differ across ethnic groups. She wonders whether she should have a conversation with Clarice about her choice of clothing and how she might be perceived.

Discussion Questions

1. Do you think Ms. Winnie should talk to Clarice about body image?
2. Would such a discussion be different if Ms. Winnie and Clarice are from the same ethnic group? From different ethnic groups?

Extending Activities

- Discuss the implications of having a dress code and its rationale.
- Discuss the implications of adopting school uniforms.
- Discuss how Ms. Winnie's unstated beliefs might impact her interaction with Clarice, Oakley, and other students.
- Discuss how educators can be more sensitive to differing perceptions of dress and body image.
- Discuss the issue of body shaming in school, whether by students or educators.

From the Evidence Vault

Ansari, A., Shepard, M., & Gottfried, M. A. (2022). School uniforms and student behavior: Is there a link? *Early Childhood Research Quarterly, 58*, 278.

In the News

Pendharkar, E. (2022, October). School dress codes aren't fair to everyone, federal study finds. *Education Week.* https://www.edweek.org/leadership/school-dress-codes-arent-fair-to-everyone-federal-study-finds/2022/10

Zaidil, S. (2022, March). Bullying and body shaming at schools, its effects and prevention. *Oladoc.* https://oladoc.com/health-zone/bullying-and-body-shaming-at-schools-its-effects-and-prevention/

Teaching Notes

Different ethnic groups have different conceptions about appropriate clothes and body image. For example, a Caucasian teacher may fail to recognize that black students may have curvier bodies than other students. Or a teacher may fail to recognize the difference in maturation rates across students and the impact on what they feel comfortable wearing.

Ms. Winnie may have shown evidence of confirmation bias in her assumptions about Clarice. Clarice may be an outstanding athlete, regardless of her physique, whereas Ms. Winnie may assume wrongly that the physical attributes would hinder her ability.

Body shaming could be across ethnic groups or within the same group. Every student is different and develops at a different rate. In middle school, it is not uncommon to see students who develop early or others who are delayed. Take, for example, tall, mature girls. Some boys have not caught up; their voices have not changed, and they have not had growth spurts. Establishing a dress code or adopting school uniforms must be considered carefully. Educators must be sensitive to the differences, especially as this time of student maturation. It is also important that students, not just the educators, are accepting of such differences.

Ethics

Body shaming is unacceptable behavior. Educators should not look at students and make an assumption about them because of their physical attributes. Educators must be vigilant to protect students. In multi-ethnic schools, educators must be especially aware of how different ethnic groups perceive body types, especially in a culture where so much emphasis is placed on overly slender individuals. Further, confirmation bias as a practice is unacceptable, whether about physical attributes, cognitive skills, or other student characteristics.

CRDL is fundamental here. Educators must be culturally sensitive and respectful. Differences exist, and they must be accepted within an asset model and whole child approach.

References and Resources

U.S. Government Accountability Office. (2022). *Department of Education should provide information on equity and safety in school dress codes* (GAO-23–105348). https://www.gao.gov/assets/gao-23-105348.pdf

Nickerson, R. S. (1998). Confirmation bias: A ubiquitous phenomenon in many guises. *Review of General Psychology, 2*(2), 175–220.

Pavlakis, A., & Roegman, R. (2018, September). How dress codes criminalize males and sexualize females of color. *PDK, 100*(2). https://www.edweek.org/leadership/school-dress-codes-arent-fair-to-everyone-federal-study-finds/2022/10

REFERRALS

Learning Objectives

- Recognize that different cultures have different acceptable behavioral patterns.
- Recognize that imposing one's cultural view on others may lead to inaccurate interpretations.

Scenario Narrative

Rusty and Thor are students at Macgregor Elementary School. They are often together at recess and on the playground. They are friends. One day on the playground, Mr. Beau witnesses the two students playing roughly. In fact, Mr. Beau perceives the two to be overly aggressive, engaging in hostile fighting. He goes to break up the altercation and without hesitation brings the two students to the office.

Mr. Bob, the principal, talks to the two boys, who are visibly upset. They try to explain to him that they were "play fighting." The boys further explain that there was no aggression or bad intent in their actions. They boys are excused, and Mr. Bob speaks to Mr. Beau about what he observed. There is an obvious difference in interpretations.

Discussion Questions

1. How might ethnic perspectives distort what Mr. Beau observed?
2. At what level is play fighting confused with real aggression?

Extending Activities

- Discuss how observations can be skewed by not understanding different cultures' acceptable behavior.
- Discuss the balance between what one ethnic group might deem appropriate behavior and what may border on violations of school policy.
- Discuss how schools can create policies that take into consideration cultural norms.

From the Evidence Vault

Parry, W. (2010, August). Battling the boys: Educators grapple with violent play. *Live Science*. https://www.livescience.com/8514-battling-boys-educators-grapple-violent-play.html

Pellis, S. M., & Pellis, V. C. (1996). On knowing it's only play: The role of play signals in play fighting. *Aggression and Violent Behavior, 1*(3), 249–268.

Teaching Notes

Mr. Beau may have been imposing his criteria for acceptable behavior on students who were engaged in behavior that is not only part of their culture but also a known phenomenon in development. Yet, the behavior may have crossed the line in terms of acceptable levels of aggression according to school policy. Part of the issue here is determining what is acceptable behavior at school. There could have been bias or profiling, either conscious or unconscious, in Mr. Beau's interpretation of what he saw. How might his observation, interpretation, and level of tolerance differ depending on the ethnicity or gender of the students?

Ethics

Observations across cultures can be skewed, causing inaccurate interpretations. There is a need for an equity lens to help educators better understand and more accurately discern which actions are acceptable in other cultures. However, some of these behaviors may be unacceptable under school policy and, therefore, require a level of explanation and cultural sensitivity. Context and background are important. Educators should attempt to gain an understanding before jumping to conclusions that might lead to inaccurate or even biased interpretations. This means using an equity lens and collecting data that can provide a broader context.

References and Resources

Legg, T. J. (2020, August). Play fighting: Should you be concerned? *Healthline.* https://www.healthline.com/health/childrens-health/play-fighting

MENTAL HEALTH

Learning Objectives

- Recognize obvious and nonobvious signs of mental illness or distress.
- Understand how to use a variety of indicators to identify students who are struggling and are having issues.

Scenario Narrative

Ms. Leena is a teacher at Polo High School. She has observed many of her students acting out. They do not seem to be engaged in their work. They often fall asleep in class. Some skip class completely. Student behavior is manifested in many ways. Ms. Leena sometimes sees students who look distressed, withdrawn, or are overly aggressive. She has watched students throw desks and chairs. She has observed signs of self-harm. She has seen students pull out their hair or eyelashes. She has seen students injure other students. She has seen students throw food, books, and other objects. The escalation of student behavioral incidents at Polo is noticeable. Ms. Leena, her colleagues, and administrators have discussed this trend and are extremely concerned. Oftentimes, it is unclear whether the behavior is a justice issue, a minor infraction, or a call for help because of underlying mental health problems, or a combination. Educators are mandated reporters; therefore, they are obligated to report issues such as abuse or neglect of their students. The behavioral manifestations may or may not reflect abuse or neglect, but they may indicate other underlying issues.

Discussion Questions

1. What does it mean for a teacher to be a mandated reporter?
2. What should Ms. Leena do with her observations of the struggling students?

Extending Activities

- Discuss how different data points can help educators identify students in danger.
- Discuss what kinds of indicators educators might use to provide evidence about struggling students.
- Discuss what kinds of actions or interventions you might use, depending on the severity of the behavior.

From the Evidence Vault

Singer, M. I., & Flannery, D. J. (2000). The relationship between children's threats of violence and violent behaviors. *Archives of Pediatrics & Adolescent Medicine, 154*(8), 785–790.

In the News

Rosales, J. (2019, June). Threatened and attacked by students: When work hurts. *NEA Today*. https://www.nea.org/advocating-for-change/new-from-nea/threatened-and-attacked-students-when-work-hurts

Teaching Notes

Behavioral issues exhibited at schools have increased substantially. The manifestation of anxiety, abuse, or mental health issues has become more challenging, more frequent, and more complex. Students react to the loss of a family member, a friend, or a teacher. Students observe violence and react. Students may manifest signs of anxiety in a variety of ways. They may cut themselves or do other forms of self-harm. They may show signs of domestic (verbal or physical) abuse. They may fear gang violence. Student may manifest their issues by flipping desks, attacking other students, or simply isolating themselves in class or the cafeteria. Today there are so many triggers for students. It is a great deal to ask of educators, but they must be observant and vigilant, and if they suspect problems, they are mandated to report them.

Protecting students from other students, from self-harm, and from educators can be tricky. It is important for educators to be aware of the regulations that prescribe what actions they can take if a student begins to act out or become violent. For example, can a teacher grab a student who is an obvious threat to other students through violent behavior? What should a teacher do if a student starts acting aggressively and the fear is that other students may be harmed?

Ethics

At times acting on the urge to protect students may violate local or state regulations. Educators must be versed in their codes of ethics, conduct, and regulations. That said, being vigilant by observing and collecting diverse data sources may help, in some cases, to prevent the manifestation of aggression, violence, or other antisocial behavior. Teachers are the frontline in noting when students may be experiencing distress, and they must report it. Data points may be subtle or obvious. They must be taken seriously to protect the welfare of the student and the classroom.

References and Resources

Many states and districts have resources to guide educators in the regulations that pertain to dealing with student mental health, aggression, violence, and other issues.

Arizona Department of Education. (2022, June). *Arizona compilation of school discipline laws and regulations.* https://safesupportivelearning.ed.gov/sites/default/files/discipline-compendium/Arizona School Discipline Laws and Regulations.pdf

Behavioral Health Services. (2019, November). *How crisis plans help schools handle violent and aggressive behavior.* https://mypts.com/blog/behavioral-health-services/how-schools-handle-violent-aggressive-students/

Pennsylvania State Education Association. (2018, September). *Dealing with threats or violent behaviors from students with IEPs.* https://www.psea.org/globalassets/for-members/professional-practice/special--gifted-education/files/dealing-with-threats-or-violent-behaviors-from-students-with-ieps.pdf

BODY SHAMING AND BULLYING

Learning Objectives

- Learn about being sensitive to students who do not conform to the norm in terms of physical attributes.
- Gain an appreciation for sensitivity toward students whose physical attributes may garner ridicule from other students.
- Learn to detect subtle forms of bullying based on untraditional data points.

Scenario Narrative

Hazel Middle School often has coed gym classes, in part to diminish gender differences in athletic participation. Building leaders believe this is a way to establish better cooperation among students as well as empathy for those who are less skilled. There is coed swimming, track, soccer, and some other sports. The intent is a good one. Teachers try to motivate students by posting time sheets, number of laps run or swam, number of chin-ups, and other relevant metrics. Students can pretty much tell which student is which. One student becomes known as Lilly Lead Butt. Another student becomes known as Bubba the Whale. A third as Harvey the Heifer. A fourth as Twinkle Toes Twyla. And another is Sammy the Snail. Students can be vicious. The teachers get wind of the derogatory comments and discuss how to handle the situation.

Discussion Questions

1. To what extent do you think posting the performance metrics led to the heckling?
2. Do you think the heckling would have occurred without the performance lists?

Extending Activities

- Discuss how using performance metrics may or may not impact students positively or negatively.
- Explore how a supposed motivational strategy can instead have unintended negative consequences.
- Discuss what the teachers could do at various stages of this scenario (e.g., posting metrics, learning about the continued taunting).
- Discuss what to do about the use of the harmful nicknames and the role of coed classes and posted performance metrics. Would the nicknames be used in single-sex classes or if performance metrics were not posted?

From the Evidence Vault

Gam, R. T., Singh, S. K., et al. (2020). Body shaming among school-going adolescents: Prevalence and predictors. *International Journal of Community Medicine and Public Health, 7*(4), 1324–1328.

In the News

Spiegler, J. (2022, August). How a Texas teen turned bias and body-shaming into advocacy and action. *Education Week.* https://www.edweek.org/leadership/opinion-how-a-texas-teen-turned-bias-and-body-shaming-into-advocacy-and-action/2022/08

Teaching Notes

Students come in different shapes and sizes. Particularly in middle school, development is manifested differently across students. All teachers, not just physical education teachers, should be keenly aware that students who do not fit the mold can be sources of ridicule and even bullying. Developmental issues might include rapid maturation, slow maturation, excessive body hair, being overweight, being too thin, wearing thick glasses, having a speech impediment, exhibiting dermatological issues, having body odor, and more. In physical education classes, some physical attributes may be detrimental to students' performance. For example:

- an overweight student who is unable to run fast or do chin-ups;
- a student who lacks the agility and gracefulness to complete a gymnastics event;

- a student with thick, corrective lenses who cannot see well enough to hit a ball;
- a student who lacks hand-eye coordination to play baseball, basketball, or other sports; or
- a student who has excessive body hair or is overweight who does not want to be seen in a bathing suit for swimming.

Heckling and ridicule can lead to something more severe such as bullying. Educators must be aware of the warning signs based on observational data. They must encourage students to be sensitive to others.

Ethics

Educators need to protect students in situations where bullying may occur and report it to leaders. Many students are vulnerable and self-conscious about their physical attributes or lack of prowess in physical activities. Not every student has the "perfect" body or is a superb athlete. Educators need to curtail derogatory terms that may diminish students' self-worth and confidence. In terms collecting and displaying data, educators should be aware of the impact of publicly posting running times, number of laps, or other metrics that would show differential performance. They should exhibit caution in communicating with students.

References and Resources

Hope, H. (2020, November). You might be body shaming your students without realizing it. *Dance Teacher*. https://dance-teacher.com/body-shaming-dance-students/

HUG THERAPY

Learning Objectives

- Learn that creativity in considering certain metrics can be an effective strategy.
- Understand that not all data must be quantitative; some may be qualitative. Some data may be more locally relevant than others.

Scenario Narrative

Gentoo Elementary School has had difficulty obtaining timely data about students' socio-emotional well-being. Standardized surveys failed to provide actionable information. Further, the results of the surveys that the state administered were significantly delayed, causing questions about their validity as they were a snapshot from some months back.

An interesting discussion occurred during a recent faculty meeting that uncovered a potentially creative metric for how students are feeling. The suggestion came from the school nurse, Ms. Elsie, rather than the teachers, but they acknowledged that it makes sense. Ms. Elsie calls the metric "hug therapy." She explained that many students who are experiencing anxiety, concerns, or just do not feel right, come into her office and simply need attention or caring—sometimes even in the form of a hug. The causes vary. It could be because of an incident at home or in school. It may be because the student is feeling anxious or ill. Or it may be something else, like needing a bit of reassurance from a caring adult.

Discussion Questions

1. Do you think that the "hug" metric is a valid indicator of a student's socio-emotional well-being?
2. To what extent should or can Ms. Elsie share with the teaches a student's outreach to her?

Extending Activities

- Discuss the concept of using proxy indicators such as the "hug" metric versus a more standardized measure such as a survey.
- Discuss the legitimacy of proxy measures more generally.
- Discuss your views about the appropriateness of school staff providing such a caring level of reassurance to students in need.

From the Evidence Vault

Furlong, M. J., Dowdy, E., et al. (2021, February). Enhancement and standardization of a universal social-emotional health measure for students' psychological strengths. *Journal of Well-Being Assessment, 4*, 245–267.

In the News

van Staaten, L. (2022, October). To improve students' mental health, schools take a team approach. *New York Times.* https://www.nytimes.com/2022/10/06/education/learning/student-mental-health-crew.html

Teaching Notes

Students are complex and manifest issues in a variety of ways. It is almost like educators must wear multiple hats, including social worker, behaviorist, and more to make sure of students' well-being, not just their academic performance. A lesson learned during the pandemic has been that for students to achieve academically, fundamental needs must be addressed. Take, for example, the Vermont Agency of Education's (2021) recovery plan, which included three pillars of recovery. The agency realized that to address the third pillar, student performance, two foundational ones must precede it. The first was attendance, truancy, and engagement. The second was the socio-emotional well-being and trauma of both students and teachers.

Standardized measures may not do justice to and reflect a given situation; that is, they may not be locally valid. In addition, standardized measures may not be the only indicator of a construct such as socio-emotional well-being. There may be a need for creative measures as well as the triangulation of multiple measures. That said, there may be district regulations about school personnel touching a student, a concern for sure.

Ethics

A first issue from this scenario is the validity of different measures of a construct, such as socio-emotional well-being. Are standardized surveys valid for this population? What about the effect of time? Certainly, students seeking reassurance can be seen as a cry for help—sometimes serious; at other times, less so. A timely response is needed. One can argue that the "hug" metric might be creative, timely, and an authentic indicator of a student's need. School policy may prevent physical contact. Parents might take exception to the contact as well. But the point here is that educators should look for creative indicators that provide insights into students who may be experiencing issues around well-being.

References and Resources

U.S. Department of Education. (n.d.). *Supporting child and student social, emotional, behavioral, and mental health needs.* https://www2.ed.gov/documents/students/supporting-child-student-social-emotional-behavioral-mental-health.pdf

Vermont Agency of Education. (2021). *Vermont's education recovery: Framework and overview.* https://education.vermont.gov/sites/aoe/files/documents/edu-framework-vermonts-education-recovery.pdf

SELF-HARM OR ABUSE

Learning Objectives

- Learn about diverse data sources and how they can provide important information about a student.
- Understand how astute observations can serve as important sources of information.
- Understand mandated reporting.

Scenario Narrative

Dulci is a seventh-grade student at Grady Middle School. She is a good student and quite social. Lately, Dulci has been appearing at school with long-sleeve clothing despite the temperature being rather warm. She also wears a long-sleeve T-shirt for gym class. A fellow student notices marks on Dulci's arms as she changes clothes and is unsure what to do. Emma questions whether she should approach Dulci or go to a teacher. Emma is concerned for her friend, so she decides to talk to a teacher known for her sensitivity. She approaches Ms. Kenya and describes what she has seen.

Ms. Kenya considers what she should do with Emma's information. She decides to observe Dulci more closely. Indeed, she seems to be covering up something on her arms. Ms. Kenya asks other teachers and the school nurse about their observations and then decides to approach Dulci. With great sensitivity, Ms. Kenya asks Dulci if she is all right. Dulci looks apprehensive, even withdrawn and upset, but she grudgingly lifts one sleeve to expose deep cuts. Ms. Kenya also observes deep bruises. It is unclear whether Dulci has cut herself or has been abused, or both.

Discussion Questions

1. What actions should Ms. Kenya take?
2. What role does Ms. Kenya have as a mandated reporter?

Extending Activities

- Suppose that Dulci does not show Ms. Kenya her arm, and all Ms. Kenya has is suspicions based on her observations and comments by the students. Discuss what actions should be taken.
- Discuss what kinds of data need to be collected and what the role of a mandated reporter is in the case of students in harm's way.
- Discuss possible actions depending on whether the situation involves abuse, self-harm, or both.

From the Evidence Vault

Ainsworth, F. (2022). Mandatory reporting of child abuse and neglect: Does it really make a difference. *Child and Family Social Work, 7*(1), 57–63.

In the News

Hixenbaugh, M., Khimm, S., & Phillip, A. (2022, October). Mandatory reporting was supposed to stop severe child abuse. It punishes poor families instead. *NBC News.* https://www.nbcnews.com/news/us-news/child-abuse-mandatory-reporting-laws-rcna50715

Teaching Notes

Mandated reporting pertains to suspected child abuse and neglect, but it also can focus on self-harm. Vigilance is required to observe students who may be experiencing any or all these situations. In most states, educators are required to report potential harm to authorities even if it is suspected and through private communication with a student.

Ms. Kenya has observed potential harm and/or abuse and it has been reported to her by other students. Ms. Kenya's interaction with Dulci is cause for legitimate concern for her well-being. The data are real from various sources and must be reported so appropriate actions can be taken.

Ethics

Educators must use care and sensitivity to protect students from potential or suspected harm. If there are any suspicions, educators must act as mandated reporters, with or without concrete evidence. Of course, having such evidence is better. That said, educators should not be overzealous but should maintain a level of observational diligence, looking for signs of changed behavior, physical issues such as bruises or cuts, and emotional effects. Withholding such information or failing to report the observations can have potentially harmful consequences for a child at risk.

References and Resources

Children's Bureau, ACYF, ACF, & HHS. (2019). *Mandatory reporters of child abuse and neglect.* https://www.childwelfare.gov/pubpdfs/manda.pdf

OVERLOOKING SOCIO-EMOTIONAL WELL-BEING

Learning Objectives

- Understand the need to look at diverse data sources, not just student performance indices.
- Understand that students need to feel emotionally stable to be positioned to learn.

Scenario Narrative

Twins Fred and Ethel are at Joseph Elementary School. Their parents both own a horse farm and work away from the farm. During the pandemic, the twins did not see any of their friends in person. All interactions were done on Zoom. They tended the animals, did their classes virtually, and tried to stay connected with their friends. There was a good deal of tension at home due to the isolation. In addition, the twins' mother was very ill for some months due to COVID. The twins had to assume more responsibility for caring for the animals, though they still maintained decent grades. But when the lockdown ended and students were allowed back in school, it was clear that the twins were withdrawn and sullen. Mr. Sophie, their teacher, keenly sensed that something was not right. She approached the twins and met with their parents.

Discussion Questions

1. Why is understanding students' socio-emotional well-being important?
2. What data are relevant to understanding socio-emotional well-being?

Extending Activities

- Discuss what kinds of indices might relate to the construct.
- Describe how you might use such indices to make decisions to help the students.
- Discuss the relationship between academic performance and socio-emotional well-being.

From the Evidence Vault

Education Northwest. (2018). *What the research says on supporting the social and emotional well-being of students.* https://educationnorthwest.org/resources/what-research-says-supporting-social-and-emotional-well-being-students

In the News

Prothero, A. (2021, March). The pandemic will affect students' mental health for years to come. How schools can help. *Education Week.* https://www.edweek.org/leadership/the-pandemic-will-affect-students-mental-health-for-years-to-come-how-schools-can-help/2021/03

Teaching Notes

Socio-emotional well-being is important for students to function effectively; it has is a direct relationship to academic performance. When students such as Fred and Ethel show evidence of some sort of emotional trauma, it is important for educators to identify the issue and find ways to address it. The root causes are likely to involve home circumstance that may require bringing in social service agencies to provide additional resources and assistance.

Ethics

Ignoring indicators of emotional struggles is problematic. For students to thrive academically, they must be in a good place emotionally. Ignoring the affective side of students and only focusing on the cognitive component can present issues. Educators must be attentive to possible traumas that may negatively impact students' emotional well-being. Teachers must be alert and know what action steps can be taken to better understand students' situations without violating their privacy and confidentiality.

References and Resources

Jones, S. M., Brush, K. E., et al. (2021). *Navigating SEL from the inside out.* https://www.wallacefoundation.org/knowledge-center/Documents/navigating-social-and-emotional-learning-from-the-inside-out-2ed.pdf

MOUTHING WHILE SINGING

Learning Objectives

- Understand the importance of working with less-talented students in a sensitive manner.
- Recognize that data and their characteristics differ based on the content area being taught.
- Understand the need to use diverse data sources about performance as well as behavior.

Scenario Narrative

Ms. Stella teaches music at River Middle School. She is very proud of the way she engages students around music, even students who are not particularly talented or interested. Ms. Stella is preparing her classes for an upcoming concert in which each class will be rated on their performance. One day, Ms. Stella discovers some students commenting on Jinx's attempt to sing, worried that Jinx will mess up the class's chance to do well in the competition. Other students, in particular Harley and CC, were highly critical of Jinx's lack of ability to sing on key. They were mean and even told Jinx to mouth the words to the songs, not sing out loud. Jinx, who was really trying, was visibly upset. Ms. Stella follows up to try to understand the problem and determines that Jinx is tone deaf. But the competition is coming up soon.

Discussion Questions

1. What should Ms. Stella do upon hearing that the students are behaving harshly toward Jinx?
2. What should Ms. Stella do in terms of Jinx?
3. Does being in a competition make any difference in what should happen instructionally or behaviorally; for example, would having Jinx mouth the words for the competition be a short-term fix?

Extending Activities

- Discuss how you think the situation should best be handled in terms of what is happening to Jinx, the behavior of the other students, and how Ms. Stella should respond instructionally to help Jinx.
- Discuss which data Ms. Stella should use to decide an appropriate course of action.
- Discuss the potential harm to Jinx in terms of performance, motivation, and emotion.
- Discuss what differences might exist if the class were an academic one and students were taunting another student over performance.

From the Evidence Vault

Conway, C., ed. (2020). *Collecting, Analyzing and Reporting Data: An Oxford Handbook of Qualitative Research in American Music Education* (vol. 2). Oxford University Press.

Forshaw, L. (2018, Fall). Don't sing, just mouth the words: How being silenced shaped a philosophy and pedagogy of inclusion. *Canadian Music Educator, 60*(1). https://go.gale.com/ps/i.do?id=GALE%7CA573714063&sid=googleScholar&v=2.1&it=r&linkaccess=abs&issn=00084549&p=AONE&sw=w&userGroupName=anon%7Ec77228a4

Schmidt, M. (2014). Collecting and analyzing observation of music teaching and learning data. C. Conway (Ed.). In *Collecting, Analyzing and Reporting Data: An Oxford Handbook of Qualitative Research in American Music Education* (pp. 227–249). Oxford University Press. https://doi.org/10.1093/oxfordhb/9780199844272.013.013

In the News

From the Front of the Choir. (2014, March 17). *Never tell someone they can't sing—it is brutal, damaging and untrue.* https://blog.chrisrowbury.com/2014/03/never-tell-someone-they-cant-sing-it-is.html

Teaching Notes

This scenario, although set in music class, can be generalized to other content areas. It highlights several issues. First, a student is not performing well in a class. How should Ms. Stella diagnose the issue and find positive, actionable steps to help her succeed? Which data are appropriate to use here to make the diagnosis? One could ask, has Ms. Stella noticed Jinx's performance lacking prior to the heckling incident? If yes, why has she not done anything? If no, then which data points should she have been using to be more observant or vigilant in assessing the student? Could Ms. Stella find instructional strategies that will tap into Jinx's interests and motivation that may lead to an improved situation? Or is Jinx truly tone deaf, and what appropriate instructional strategies could be taken? All of these are good questions.

Second, how should Ms. Stella handle Harley, CC, and the other students who have criticized Jinx? This is a class management issue and potentially a bullying situation. Students making fun of less-talented students for their mistakes is highly problematic. It can lead to permanent harm and negative consequences.

Third, consider which data points should be examined to inform the decision making in terms of instruction, behavior, and classroom management.

Ethics

If intended, the group of students were heckling Jinx, so Ms. Stella must take appropriate action to stop this behavior. Ms. Stella should manage her class in a way that accommodates all students across the spectrum of abilities. She might speak with Jinx to tap into her interests, which may lead to specific instructional strategies to improve her performance. At no time should Ms. Stella single out Jinx about how poorly she sings. Such action would only further embarrass her, possibly leading to permanent dislike of music and emotional distress.

Ms. Stella also needs to handle the situation with the other students. Their behavior is unacceptable, tantamount to bullying. She may want to see if these students behave similarly toward Jinx in other settings, not just music class. Ms. Stella may also want to inquire subtly whether Jinx is struggling in other settings as well or if it is only because she simply cannot sing. The main concern here, however, is to protect Jinx, her privacy, and ensure that she is not being harassed by other students.

Ms. Stella might have dealt only with Jinx's issue of tone deafness, rather than also addressing the impact of the subtle bullying without considering the full range of data. In this case, performance and emotional data as well as observations can provide a deeper understanding of the situation. Without a broad perspective of the situation, Ms. Stella may see only isolated, unconnected issues, which obviously is not the case.

References and Resources

Conway, C., ed. (2020). *Collecting, Analyzing and Reporting Data: An Oxford Handbook of Qualitative Research in American Music Education* (vol. 2). Oxford University Press.

Culp, M. E., & Jones, M. K. (2020). Shame in music education: Starting the conversation and developing resilience. *Music Educators Journal, 106*(6).

SILENCE

Learning Objectives

- Understand how to look for the nonobvious and to look between the lines.
- Understand the importance of nonverbal clues and observations that may lead to explanations about students' behavior and performance.
- Understand how to look at the broad picture of a classroom, taking in both explicit and less explicit cues about students.

Scenario Narrative

Pippa is a student at Moses Middle School. Pippa has always been an engaged student. She willingly raises her hand to answer questions. She is known for being really smart and getting good grades but not being smug about knowing the answers.

Pippa is in a social studies class led by Ms. Luna. Ms. Luna is conducting a class in which there is a teaming exercise as well as whole-class participation. Ms. Luna circulates among the groups and notices that Pippa has not said much of anything in the group setting. In fact, she seems almost withdrawn and reticent to say anything. She is not engaging and pretty much is just sitting in the group. She is, however, paying attention. When Ms. Luna convenes back into the whole class, she notices again that Pippa has not said a thing. She asks a question of the group to which she knows Pippa has the answer, yet she does not respond. Other students provide answers. Ms. Luna starts calling on various students and then looks at Pippa directly. Ms. Luna is stumped by such a drastic change in Pippa. She asks her to stay after class to discuss.

Scenario 1. The description ends.

Scenario 2. The description continues.

Ms. Luna asks Pippa what is going on. The response surprises her. Indeed, Pippa knows the answers, but she refuses to speak up in class because other students have begun mocking her every time she raises her hand or begins to speak. After several attempts, Pippa has been bullied into silence. She is no longer willing to speak up because other students are calling her names about being too smart, the teacher's pet, and even worse. Pippa bursts into tears. Through the negative conditioning she does not want to show her knowledge in front of other students.

Discussion Questions

1. As a teacher, how would you interpret Pippa's silence?
2. What would you do to try to stimulate Pippa to respond?
3. As a teacher, do you have awareness of the circumstances around Pippa's silence?

Extending Activities

- Discuss possible explanations for why a student such as Pippa has stopped volunteering to speak up in class.
- Describe what activities you might use to draw Pippa out.
- Discuss what actions you would take, upon learning of the bullying situation toward Pippa, toward the students mocking her.

From the Evidence Vault

Zakrajsek, T. (2017, April). Students who don't participate in class discussions: They are not all introverts. *Scholarly Teacher*. https://www.scholarlyteacher.com/post/students-who-dont-participate-in-class-discussions

Teaching Notes

Bullying can be subtle. It does not have to be physical. In this situation, Pippa has been bullied into silence through no fault of her own. The bullying here may have been so subtle that Ms. Luna did not even notice it. She did, however, notice the dramatic change in Pippa's behavior. Ms. Luna's probing provides concrete evidence that something yet unknown is happening with a student in trouble. She questioned the situation. Luckily, Pippa felt comfortable confiding in Ms. Luna what was happening. But what if Pippa had remained silent, and the bullying continued? Pippa would continue to withdraw further with the distinct possibility of harmful consequences. Teachers must be diligent about the unspoken, the less obvious cues that occur in the classroom. Perhaps in this instance, Ms. Luna missed cues of how students were mocking Pippa. Perhaps they were pretty adept at hiding the behavior. A continuation of this kind of mocking could easily have a lasting effect on any student, well beyond their academic years.

Ethics

The main issue in this scenario is that the bullying from the students has caused Pippa to stop responding. She has clammed up. The observation of the bullying is key here as it has led to Pippa's response. Ms. Luna must deal with those students as well as helping Pippa to overcome her resistance to responding in class. The long-term ramifications of being mocked for responding can be substantial.

If Ms. Luna uses the observational data and her knowledge of Pippa's long-term performance, she will discern that something is amiss and try to identify the problem. If Ms. Luna fails to notice the bullying, then she may make a completely different interpretation about why Pippa no longer responds in class. The triangulation of the data sources will make an important difference in understanding the nuances of the situation.

References and Resources

Amaro, M. (n.d.). 10 ways to deal with a student who won't engage. *Highly Effective Teacher*. https://thehighlyeffectiveteacher.com/10-ways-to-deal-with-a-student-who-wont-engage/

Psych4schools. (2017, October). *Students who don't speak up in class*. https://www.psych4schools.com.au/blog/speakupclass/

ATTENDANCE AND CHRONIC ABSENCES

Learning Objectives

- Understand that there are many ways to measure attendance.
- Help educators acquire more accurate measures of attendance to take into consideration students' needs.

Scenario Narrative

Mr. Nugget is a vice principal responsible for charting attendance at Bailey High School. During the pandemic, students were expected to attend class virtually. Measuring attendance was challenging in the virtual environment. It was difficult to discern whether students were online and attending. Once Bailey retuned to in-person instruction, determining attendance remained a challenge. Younger students who were not socialized into moving from class to class did not understand that they were expected to show up in class each period. The students might be "in school," meaning on the campus, but they often did not attend class. Attendance data, therefore, were fraught with errors. Given that attendance in this high school was factored into performance metrics, students found that they were being penalized by individual teachers. Mr. Nugget hoped that this trend would be transient after things stabilized following the pandemic.

Another residual effect from the pandemic was seen in Bailey's feeder schools, Elsie Middle School and Ollie Elementary School. Many students have been deemed chronically absent, using the 10% absentee rate as the criterion. Students who miss at least 18 of the 180 school days are considered chronically absent, and actions are taken with these students. Part of the reason students are not attending is that they have become accustomed to not coming to school in the wake of the pandemic. Students learned virtually and did not have interactions with classmates. Coming to school physically also introduced for some students a fear of being with other children. Students are staying home because they are sad, fearful, have anxieties, or simply cannot easily get to school. Mr. Watson, the principal, analyzed data to discern trends in the chronic absentee data. He found a disproportionate number of low-income students and students of color falling behind due to their absences. The feeder schools have instituted incentive programs to try to mitigate the attendance and absentee issues.

Discussion Questions

1. How do you think attendance data should be collected to be fair to the students and the teacher?
2. What do you think about having multiple indicators of the attendance variable? Does this make sense to you?
3. What do you think the feeder schools should do?

Extending Activities

- Discuss why having a reliable, valid measure of attendance is important in education.
- Explore how attendance as a data point may work against certain students.
- Discuss why you think the chronic absentee issue disproportionately impacts low-income students and students of color.
- Discuss the kinds of incentives that might be put in place to mitigate chronic absenteeism.

From the Evidence Vault

McConnell, B. M., & Kubina, R. M., Jr. (2014). Connecting with families to improve students' school attendance: A review of the literature. *Preventing School Failure: Alternative Education for Children and Youth, 58*(4), 249–256.

In the News

Fortin, J. (2022, April). More pandemic fallout: The chronically absent student. *New York Times*. https://www.nytimes.com/2022/04/20/us/school-absence-attendance-rate-covid.html

Gonzalez, D. (2023, March). Chronic absenteeism soared during the pandemic. Here's why Arizona students still aren't going to school. *Arizona Republic*. https://www.azcentral.com/story/news/local/arizona-education/2023/03/21/arizona-students-still-arent-going-to-school-post-covid-19/69960399007/

Teaching Notes

Students are expected to attend school. It is the law. Schools and districts are expected to report accurate attendance data for compliance purposes. Yet, the measurement of attendance is not always straightforward, and the variable can be calculated multiple ways. Attendance often appears in a student's permanent record, so it is important to be as accurate as possible. Districts also rely on the accuracy of attendance data; they must report it to their state education agency, which, in turn, reports it to the U.S. Department of Education for accountability purposes. At the high-school level, students move from class to class, so the calculation is for attendance in a class period, but a concern is whether a student fails to attend one or more classes that day. District and building administrators need to be clear and consistent in their definition of attendance. They need to communicate expectations and definitions to faculty, students, and parents to minimize misunderstandings about what it means to be in school.

According to various studies, "disadvantaged" students are more likely to be deemed chronically absent (Barat et al., 2021, 2022). The reasons are varied. They include transportation issues, disengagement with school, bullying, instability at home, and a lack of understanding of the impact of missing school. Missing school for these students further widens achievement disparities because it is hard to learn if you are not in school. This becomes a downward cycle as students fall farther and farther behind. One strategy that can be used is having students track their own absence data and take ownership for those data. This way, they can recognize when they might be at risk. Such an activity might help bring awareness to the students and, therefore, modify their behavior. Another strategy is to work directly with the student and his or her parents or guardians, even making home visits. A third strategy is rewarding or recognizing students for good attendance and publicizing good performance.

Ethics

Data elements require that they are reliable and valid to be informative. This is a fundamental principle of measurement and data literacy. The variable needs to be defined and measured in a way that helps educators make informed decisions from the data elements. If a data element is ill-defined or ambiguous in terms of the actual measurement, the potential is for misuse and harm to individual students and the educational agency. Thus, careful specification is needed.

In terms of chronic absenteeism, the flip side of attendance, it is important to understand the root causes for students who meet the criterion. It may be disengagement with the curriculum. It may be a transportation issue. It may be fear of coming to school because of bullying or another anxiety-producing situation. It may be because of circumstances in the students' homes. Some things may be within the control of the educators, but most likely are not. The important issue is to understand the situation through a variety of data sources so that educators can begin to work with the student and family and bring in external resources to help get students to school. The logic model is clear: the more students miss school, the farther they fall behind, and the greater likelihood they are at risk of dropping out. Understanding the root causes through data can help to break this negative cycle.

References and Resources

Attendance Works. (n.d.). *Resources*. https://www.attendanceworks.org/resources/

Barat, V. X., et al. (2021, October). *Chronic absenteeism in Arizona: A description of K–8 trends 2017–2021*. https://www.helios.org/media/zeckn0xp/brief-az-chronic-absence-report_final-draft_with-appendix_proofed.pdf

Barat, V. X., et al. (2022, July). *Missing too much school: Trends in K–8 chronic absenteeism in Arizona during the pandemic*. https://helios.org/media/hzydjckw/22hls024-az-chronic-absence-brief_final_digital.pdf

National Forum on Education Statistics. (2018). *Forum guide to collecting and using attendance data* (NFES-2017–007). https://nces.ed.gov/pubs2017/NFES2017007.pdf

GAMING THE SYSTEM

Learning Objectives

- Understand how manipulating data, even if the purpose is to help students, is improper practice.
- Understand how gaming the system ignores some students who also need attention.

Scenario Narrative

Mr. Rex and Mr. Dusty are teachers at Dixie Elementary School. Every year when annual testing comes around, they are faced with pressure from the administration to increase the number of students who pass the tests. The teachers know who are the high achievers, the students in the middle of the performance continuum, and those who are struggling. Some teachers feel their best bet at producing good results is to focus on the students just on the cusp of passing. They provide intensive instructional interventions to these students to get them over the passing criterion. Other teachers disagree with this strategy, claiming that every student needs at least some attention, some more than others. Mr. Rex and Mr. Dusty fall into the latter group and have a heated argument with colleagues and the administration about the strategy and the pressure they are experiencing.

Discussion Questions

1. What do you think about the strategy to focus on the "bubble students"?
2. What do you think is the recommended instructional strategy leading up to annual testing?

Extending Activities

- Discuss instructional strategies that will address students at all points on the performance continuum.
- Discuss the measurement concepts of regression to the mean and errors of measurement and how they apply to the strategy of focusing on "bubble students."

From the Evidence Vault

Booher-Jennings, J. (2005). "Educational triage" and the Texas accountability system. *American Educational Research Journal, 42*(2), 231–268.

Nichols, S. L. (2021). Educational policy contexts and the (un)ethical use of data. In E. B. Mandinach & E. S. Gummer (Eds.), *The Ethical Use of Data in Education: Promoting Responsible Policies and Practices* (pp. 81–97). Teachers College Press.

In the News

Blinder, A. (2015, April). Atlanta educators convicted in school cheating scandal. *New York Times*. https://www.nytimes.com/2015/04/02/us/verdict-reached-in-atlanta-school-testing-trial.html

Chen, G. (2023, January). When teachers cheat: The standardized test controversy. *Public School Review*. https://www.publicschoolreview.com/blog/when-teachers-cheat-the-standardized-test-controversies

Kamenetz, A. (2014, November). Testing: How much is too much? *NPRED*. https://www.npr.org/blogs/ed/2014/11/17/362339421/testing-how-much-is-too-much

Teaching Notes

Accountability pressures often cause educators to do things that are not entirely proper. Most educators act appropriately, but some buckle under pressure. Actions might be in the form of actual cheating or more subtly, gaming the system. Cheating scandals have made the news where educators have changed test answers. More often, teachers feel pressure to maximize the number of students who perform well on standardized assessments. In a well-cited article, Booher-Jennings (2005) described how teachers focused on what is called the bubble students, trying to help them over the criterion for competence or the passing cut score. In focusing solely on students just below the criterion, teachers ignore students at the far ends of the continuum or even those just above the criterion. The assumption is that the high achievers need less or no help, the lowest achievers never will succeed, and those who have already passed will stay where they are. The best bet is to try to move up those just below the cut score. Such practice is ill-advised for many reasons. Every student deserves attention, regardless of where they are along the performance continuum.

Ethics

Gaming the system goes to the heart of many of the well-publicized cheating scandals such as in Atlanta and elsewhere. Cheating has occurred in pre-college venues, in college admissions, and in higher education. The Varsity Blues cheating scandal involved parents and others paying off college coaches and administrators to gain acceptance for their children as well as paying for surrogates to take college entrance examinations. Cheating has become a creative endeavor.

In the scenario depicted here, ignoring some groups of students to focus solely on those educators assume have the greatest chance of improving is a bad instructional strategy. It is wrong to ignore high achievers, assuming they will succeed regardless of the level of attention they receive. Similarly, it is wrong to ignore the students who struggle the most, with the assumption that they will not succeed regardless. The concepts of educational measurement would say that those on either side of a passing criterion could regress as well as improve. All students need attention, based on their needs, strengths, and challenges.

References and Resources

Mandinach, E. B. & Gummer, E. S. (Eds.). (2021). *The Ethical Use of Data in Education: Promoting Responsible Policies and Practices.* Teachers College Press.

MANIPULATING PERFORMANCE

Learning Objectives

- Understand the importance of using multiple measures of performance.
- Understand the importance of working to meet the needs of every student, regardless of accountability pressures and context.

Scenario Narrative

Ms. Millie is a language arts teacher at Kapuki High School, one that always competes at the highest level for state athletic championships. She is aware that some of her students are athletes and may be eligible for college scholarships, depending on how the team does. Many of the student-athletes can make it on their own in terms of academic performance, but a few receive remedial help. One student is of particular concern. The coach, Mr. Otis, pays a visit to Ms. Millie and discusses the importance of having the student, Dallas, for an upcoming game, even though his scores are borderline or below the cut point for eligibility. Mr. Otis strongly encourages Ms. Millie to "make sure" that Dallas receives a passing grade so he can play. Not only does Ms. Millie get some not-so-subtle pressure from Mr. Otis, but also from Dallas's parents, Mr. and Mrs. Allie, because of the risk of losing possible scholarships.

Ms. Millie has a discussion with the Allies and lays out her expectations for Dallas's performance. She explains that the grade depends on multiple activities that include classroom participation, completion of assignments, and some upcoming quizzes. She is trying to give Dallas every opportunity to succeed by laying out multiple ways that he can pass without compromising her standards. She would do the same for any struggling student. But what happens if Dallas still does not pass because he has failed to show up at class, participate, or turn in assignments? The expectations were made clear.

Discussion Questions

1. What should Ms. Millie do? Consult the principal? Buckle under the pressure?
2. What do you think about athletes given an easy pass?
3. What do you think of Mr. Otis's actions?
4. What do you think should happen if Dallas fails to complete Ms. Millie's requirements?

Extending Activities

- Discuss Ms. Millie's practice of providing multiple ways for a student to demonstrate an acceptable level of performance.
- Discuss the pressure that Ms. Millie has taken from both the coach and the student's parents.

From the Evidence Vault

Nichols, S. L. (2021). Educational policy contexts and the (un)ethical use of data. In E. B. Mandinach & E. S. Gummer (Eds.), *The Ethical Use of Data in Education: Promoting Responsible Policies and Practices* (pp. 81–97). Teachers College Press.

In the News

Lavaigne, P. (2012, October). Bad grades: Some schools are okay with it. *ESPN*. https://www.espn.com/espn/otl/story/_/page/Outside-The-Lines-GPA/some-high-schools-actually-reducing-gpa-requirements-student-athletes

Lyall, S. (2013, December). A's for athletes, but charges of fraud at North Carolina. *New York Times*. https://www.nytimes.com/2014/01/01/sports/as-for-athletes-but-charges-of-tar-heel-fraud.html?searchResultPosition=3

Teaching Notes

Coaches and parents have been known to pressure teachers to ensure that star athletes are made academically eligible for their sports. Falsifying grades, changing grades, having others complete assignments for the athletes, and other strategies give an athlete a free pass and do no one any good. The way the scenario depicts Ms. Millie at least gives Dallas a pathway to succeed through using multiple measures, not just one test. She is not giving him an exception or making him a special case. Ms. Millie is using a fundamental concept of measurement and data use, which is to use multiple measures to provide evidence of learning and performance. If Dallas were to fail a quiz, it would be game over. Or if he refused to participate in class, also game over. But by providing Dallas with multiple ways to demonstrate his learning, Ms. Millie is providing a reasonable strategy for all students.

Ethics

Manipulating a teacher's grading practice for any reason is simply wrong. Mr. Otis should never have pressured Ms. Millie, nor should Dallas's parents. From a data standpoint, Ms. Millie is giving Dallas several chances to succeed, not just basing his eligibility on one activity. That is a reasonable course of action. If Dallas fails to attend class, turn in assignments, or pass quizzes, then Ms. Millie has done the right thing to mitigate the inappropriate pressure.

Such pressure does happen. There have been many public scandals at the university level as coaches pressure professors to enable athletes to play. One of the most public cheating scandals occurred at the University of North Carolina where professors were paid off, courses were taught incompletely or not at all, and the athletes were awarded good grades. The athletes in question were members of the football team. *One on One*, a movie released long ago, depicted how large universities provide tutors, fake jobs, and fake grades to basketball players.

Educators should make every effort to help their students succeed but within the boundaries of ethics. They should not be pressured to manipulate grades, forgo assignments, or falsify work. It does not help the student and is committing fraud.

References and Resources

Wretman, C. (2017). School sports participation and academic achievement in middle and high school. *Journal of the Society for Social Work and Research, 8*(3), 1–22. https://www.journals.uchicago.edu/doi/10.1086/693117

TO TEST OR NOT TO TEST

Learning Objectives

- Understand the ramifications of accountability pressures.
- Understand the differences between data for accountability and data for continuous improvement.

Scenario Narrative

Mr. Kutsy is a teacher at Luke High School. The school is in a fairly affluent suburb where there is significant pressure for high performance. Annual state testing is this week, and

Mr. Kutsy is concerned. A few of his best students have been ill and are absent. Having these good students test will help Luke's academic standing. Other teachers have a similar problem—that is, some good students are absent, yet none of the students who are struggling are absent. The concern is if the good students do not test, the results will not accurately reflect the level of achievement. The teachers receive a message via a faculty rumor mill that the administration wants to ensure that the good students are present for the testing, despite being sick, and perhaps encourage some of the less strong students to be absent. Mr. Kutsy talks to his colleagues about this rumor.

Discussion Questions

1. What do you think about the testing strategy?
2. What do you think the teachers should do?

Extending Activities

- Discuss how such requests could impact the motivation of the students.
- Explore how this strategy and others "game" the accountability system.
- Discuss the ethics of accountability pressures versus using data for continuous improvement of all students.
- Discuss the ethics of encouraging students to stay at home or come to school to increase test scores.

From the Evidence Vault

Booher-Jennings, J. (2005). "Educational triage" and the Texas accountability system. *American Educational Research Journal, 42*(2), 231–268.

Nichols, S. L. (2021). Educational policy contexts and the (un)ethical use of data. In E. B. Mandinach & E. S. Gummer (Eds.), *The Ethical Use of Data in Education: Promoting Responsible Policies and Practices* (pp. 81–97). Teachers College Press.

In the News

Samuels, C. A. (2011, August). Cheating scandals intensify focus on testing pressures. *Education Week*. https://www.edweek.org/teaching-learning/cheating-scandals-intensify-focus-on-test-pressures/2011/08

Martin, M. (2019, February). Former teacher blames education policymakers for Atlanta cheating scandal. *NPR*. https://www.npr.org/2019/02/16/695344751/former-teacher-blames-education-policymakers-for-atlanta-cheating-scandal

Teaching Notes

Gaming the testing system is simply wrong. To make a school or district look better based only on test scores, gaming gives educators a bad reputation. The public generally does not understand the nuances of what test scores mean and how they should be interpreted. They only know that higher is better. Accountability pressures abound at many levels, and often, the teachers are the pawns in the game of showing higher achievement.

Telling good students that they must be in school regardless of their health situation is bad practice just as it is to tell weaker students to coincidentally be absent. It demeans the students and can negatively impact their motivation and self-esteem. It sends the wrong message. Good students can also be bad test takers, so what should educators tell those students?

In far too many instances, educators are being forced to game the accountability system to make their school or district look better. Results are published in public media. Parents threaten to remove their children from low-performing schools. Property values can be impacted by school performance. A great deal rides on high test scores. Gaming is the wrong message to give students and educators (i.e., that such cheating is acceptable). Such gaming calls into question the purposes of the assessments, the validity of the results, and the subsequent interpretations.

Ethics

The ethics of manipulating the testing process have been a recurrent problem over time. Test scores are used to make decisions for specific and intended purposes; this is validity. The use of scores for unintended purposes brings the validity of interpretations into question. Manipulating the testing process in any way is problematic at best. Even using standardized test scores to inform instructional practice is problematic because of their alignment to the local curricula. Other ethical issues arise with the tension between addressing student needs (i.e., data for continuous improvement) and the pressure to look good to stakeholders for compliance purposes (i.e., data for accountability and compliance). Consider factoring standardized test scores into teacher evaluations, a controversial topic at best.

References and Resources

Bennett, R. E. (2011). Formative assessment: A critical review. *Assessment in Education: Principles, Policy & Practice, 18*(1), 5–25.

NUTRITION ACTIVITY

Learning Objectives

- Learn how some technology can highlight issues to help educators assist students.
- Understand how to triangulate disparate data sources to reach more accurate conclusions.

Scenario Narrative

The Roger School District created a program in which teachers at the elementary and middle schools collect data about exercise and nutrition through a technology app. Leaders at Roger are concerned about a growing issue that focuses on students who may not be receiving proper nutrition and getting enough exercise. As a consequence, some students are suffering from medical problems. The objective of the app is for students to log activities and food consumption, with the app providing analyses that might highlight good and ineffective practices. The app captures number of steps, whether the student takes the school stairs or uses the elevator, and other physical activities. The app also asks about the kinds of food eaten, frequency, and quantity as well as how the food is prepared (e.g., fried, boiled, broiled, raw, etc.). The app notes whether the food is prepared at home or purchased, such as at a fast-food establishment. It can categorize junk food, fast food, comfort food, or healthy food. Because the district serves a low-income population, a concern is that many students are not receiving a balanced diet at home, where families must resort to less healthy options due to financial constraints. Such information can help the food services staff make decisions about how to prepare nutritious meals at breakfast, lunch, and snacks.

Discussion Questions

1. What kinds of data do you expect the app might generate to help staff improve student nutrition?
2. What do you think about capturing these kinds of data?

Extending Activities

- Discuss why using such technology can help the school better address the needs of some students.
- Describe what kinds of solutions might ensue from the analytics.
- Discuss how the app might shed light on students whose home circumstances prevent them from receiving proper nutrition.
- Discuss how the information might be factored into provisions for weekend food.
- Discuss the validity of the data, based on some data input by the students.

From the Evidence Vault

Iversen, C. S., Nigg, C., & Titchenal, C. A. (2011, July). The impact of an elementary after-school nutrition and physical activity program on children's fruits and vegetable intake, physical activity, and body mass index: Fun 5. *Hawaii Medical Journal, 7*(suppl 1), 37–41.

In the News

Sack, K. (2007, October). Schools found improving on nutrition and fitness. *New York Times*. https://www.nytimes.com/2007/10/20/health/20junkfood.html

Teaching Notes

Students cannot function or learn effectively if they are hungry. Students also can suffer health issues if they do not receive proper nutrition. Oftentimes, low-income students not only do not have access to nutritional food at home, but they may go hungry over weekends because their families do not have sufficient food. Some districts have introduced food backpack programs to help students in need. Collecting data with the help of the app can provide invaluable information to the district to structure their food services. But the utility of the data is predicated on having a certain level of accuracy.

Related to proper nutrition is exercise. Some students loathe exercise and find ways to avoid it, such as using an elevator rather than taking the stairs. It is not uncommon in some affluent communities to see children using e-bikes and other motorized devices, rather than using real bikes. Elsewhere, some students may need to walk to school in bad weather conditions because they have no other transportation. Thus, the data collected from the app can also provide results about physical activity to determine whether students can improve their level of activity.

Ethics

Collecting student data through an app is a creative way of gathering information that can help the district understand important issues such as fitness and nutrition. It can inform their food services department, their physical education teachers, and school nurses. One question to consider is whether these kinds of data, as part of a school program or class, are a valid way of collecting information, or do such activities in some way violate student privacy. Do students and families need to consent to such data collection? What happens if the data collection process is inaccurate due to how the data are input? Helping students to increase their fitness and having proper food is important, but the district must balance the need for such information with the protection of student privacy.

References and Resources

Centers for Disease Control. (n.d.). Healthy eating learning opportunities and nutrition education. *CDC Healthy Schools*. https://www.cdc.gov/healthyschools/nutrition/school_nutrition_education.htm

PHYSICAL ACTIVITY

Learning Objectives

- Understand the disproportionate ramifications for low-income students of curtailing physical education classes and school sports.
- Understand the relationship between physical activity and other variables such as academic performance, self-confidence, and social-emotional well-being.

Scenario Narrative

The Maya School District has been facing a budget crisis. District administrators have faced extremely difficult decisions. Ms. Olive, the superintendent, has consulted with the financial director, Mr. Halle, as well as faculty, community members, the school board, and other stakeholders before publicly making any announcements. Leadership did not want to sacrifice academic programs. The only option was to cut back on sports teams and physical education. Mr. Taffer, the head of the physical education department, is concerned and has been trying to identify alternatives. Nonetheless, the decision was difficult. The administration considered its options and recognized that students had other options to engage in athletics outside of school because of the proliferation of clubs and teams on which children can participate. Ms. Eva, a mother of one student, raises a legitimate concern. The cost for participation on these teams is substantial, especially purchasing the needed equipment. It is possible that some or many students will be unable to participate because of financial constraints.

Discussion Questions

1. What do you think of this decision?

2. Do you think that sacrificing physical education was the right decision?

Extending Activities

- Discuss the relationship among physical activity, student performance, and self-confidence.
- Discuss how such a decision can disproportionately and negatively impact low-income students.
- Discuss the assumption that students have access to external clubs and teams.

From the Evidence Vault

Aspen Institute. (2019). *State of play: Trends and developments in youth play.* https://www.aspeninstitute.org/wp-content/uploads/2019/10/2019_SOP_National_Final.pdf

Biddle, S. J. H., & Asare, M. (2011). Physical activity and mental health in children and adolescents: A review of reviews. *British Journal of Sports Medicine, 45*(11), 886–895. https://bjsm.bmj.com/content/45/11/886.short

Black, L. I., Terlizzi, E. P., & Vahratian, A. (2022, August). *Organized sports among children aged 6–17 years: United States, 2020* (NCHS Data Brief, No. 441). https://www.cdc.gov/nchs/data/databriefs/db441.pdf

Trudeau, F., & Shepard, R. J. (2008). Physical education, school physical activity, school sports, and academic performance. *International Journal of Behavioral Nutrition and Physical Activity, 5*(10), 1–12.

In the News

Richtel, M. (2023, March). Income gap becomes a physical-activity divide. *New York Times.* https://www.nytimes.com/2023/03/24/health/sports-physical-education-children.html

Teaching Notes

Assuming or expecting that students can readily find physical activity outside school through clubs and teams is fallacious. Research has shown that the participation rate is disproportionate based on income level (see references above). Low-income students are less likely to participate than are middle- or high-income students. Thus, canceling physical education and sports activity negatively impacts some students more than others. In addition to that inequality, physical activity has been shown to positively impact academic performance, student mental health, and other factors. The decision by the district could have broader impact than simply cutting the budget for nonacademic classes and activities. It will disproportionately and unfairly disadvantage low-income students, not just in their physical activity but by the positive effects on other aspects of student functioning.

Ethics

District administrators had a difficult decision to make. It was a "Sophie's Choice." It would be difficult to argue that cutting academic courses is a good decision. The problem here, however, is whether the administrators did their due diligence to understand the potential for disproportionate impact on families that cannot afford to pay for external sports teams and clubs. They also may not have fully considered the relationship between physical activity and academic performance or with mental health. Administrators may have made the best decision based on obvious choices—academics versus sports—but the ethical issue is the extent to which they were aware of the disproportionate impact and still made the decision. Perhaps working with community organizations to provide funding for needy students so that they can participate in external sports activities might be a possible solution.

References and Resources

Centers for Disease Control. (2013). *Comprehensive school physical activity programs: A guide for schools*. https://www.cdc.gov/healthyschools/physicalactivity/pdf/13_242620-A_CSPAP_SchoolPhysActivityPrograms_Final_508_12192013.pdf

Centers for Disease Control. (n.d.). *Physical activity facts*. https://www.cdc.gov/healthyschools/physicalactivity/facts.htm

SIZE MATTERS

Learning Objectives

- Learn not to make unconscious judgments about students based on body types.
- Learn how harmful body shaming can be.

Scenario Narrative

Gracie and Olivia are sophomores at Frances High School. Both participate in the school's sports program, but teachers have different perspectives about and expectations for the two students. Teachers are also concerned about both students but for different reasons. At such a young age, Gracie weighs more than 200 pounds, yet she is agile on the playing field. The coaches and physical education teachers observe her and make assumptions about her athletic ability and even her level of effort, simply based on her size. Teachers and the school nurse also have made assumptions based on observations. They question Gracie's health and well-being, her eating habits, and whether she is receiving proper nutrition. Teachers see her struggle to fit into typical desks and into sports uniforms. It is possible that Gracie is experiencing fat shaming.

Olivia is the opposite. She is incredibly thin, almost skeletal. Teachers also worry about her nutrition. Some have questioned whether she is anorexic. Olivia is also an athlete. The physical education teachers and her coaches are concerned about whether her frail physique can withstand competition.

The educators, nurse, and school administrators confer and discuss how to handle their concerns about both students. They contact the students' parents and ask for a set of meetings.

Discussion Questions

1. Do you think these observations are valid?
2. Do you think these are cases of body shaming in either direction?
3. What do you think about having the parental meetings?
4. What do you think the educators should do?

Extending Activities

- Discuss issues around body image and body shaming in adolescents, particularly girls.
- Discuss what you think are legitimate concerns here and what, if anything, the educators should do.
- Discuss how your interpretations might differ if there were rumors about Oliva purging or Gracie consuming a lot of junk food.

From the Evidence Vault

McNinch, H. (2016). Eleven: Fat bullying of girls in elementary and secondary schools: Implications for teacher education. *Counterpoints, 467*, 113–121.

In the News

Brody, J. E. (2017, August). Fat bias starts early and takes a serious toll. *New York Times*. https://www.nytimes.com/2017/08/21/well/live/fat-bias-starts-early-and-takes-a-serious-toll.html

Fitzsimmons, E. G. (2023, April). New York considers outlawing discrimination based on weight. *New York Times*. https://www.nytimes.com/2023/04/06/nyregion/weight-discrimination-law-nyc.html

Teaching Notes

Body image, particularly for adolescent girls, is a challenging and sensitive topic. Social media and public media promote that thin is good. Girls see performers, models, athletes, and other people as role models. Yet, body types differ. The body mass index (BMI) sets expectations for the ideal based on height and weight. Medicine defines obesity as a medical condition, a disease to be addressed. Fat shaming is common. Terminology is a sensitive matter. What should be used? Fat? Obese? Overweight? Something else? Students may not fit into desks. They may not fit into sports uniforms. Fat shaming manifests itself in many ways in terms of assumptions and perceptions, such as being lazy, unkempt, eating wrong, not exercising, and so much more. Organizations such as the National Association to Advance Fat Acceptance have been created to combat misconceptions and discrimination.

Ethics

Body shaming can be related to self-esteem, confidence, and other affective variables. Body image and body shaming can be ripe for bullying. Students may well be comfortable in their own body and do not need to be reminded if they are too thin, too fat, or something else. The National Association to Advance Fat Acceptance discusses how fat people should be considered among other protected groups that face discrimination. Having the appropriate data to understand what is happening is important. Educators should not rush to judgment but, instead, do their due diligence to understand the situations of students whose body images do not conform to the "norm." The students should not be stigmatized. They should not even be designated as being unhealthy. Neutral descriptors should be found and used.

References and Resources

Dellecese, C. (2023). Eye of the tigress. *Smith Alumnae Quarterly*.
National Association to Advance Fat Acceptance. (n.d.). https://naafa.org/

Chapter 6

Change Is Systemic

THE ROLES OF ORGANIZATIONS AND AGENCIES

The adage "it takes a village" is apt here. Unfortunately, change does not come easily to education. There are many challenges and impediments to change, perhaps the most pressing being time and money. Change requires time and effort. It can also be costly. In this chapter, I take a systems perspective to examine how the roles of and the interactions among various agencies and stakeholder groups are needed to ensure that culturally responsive data literacy (CRDL) becomes embedded in education.

I identify several stakeholder groups that can have an impact on or be impacted by implementing CRDL in education. The groups include the U.S. Department of Education, state education agencies, local education agencies, professional organizations, educator preparation programs, professional development providers, and testing and licensure agencies. Figure 6.1 attempts to depict the complex interactions among these groups. This chapter will walk through each of the stakeholder groups and discuss the role they can play around CRDL.

As can be seen in figure 6.1, CRDL is at the center of the diagram, indicating that as a targeted focus of getting the construct implemented into educational practice, it is influenced by the policy context, the standards and codes, the requirements in terms of licensure and certification, and the extent to which CRDL is included in educator preparation and training.

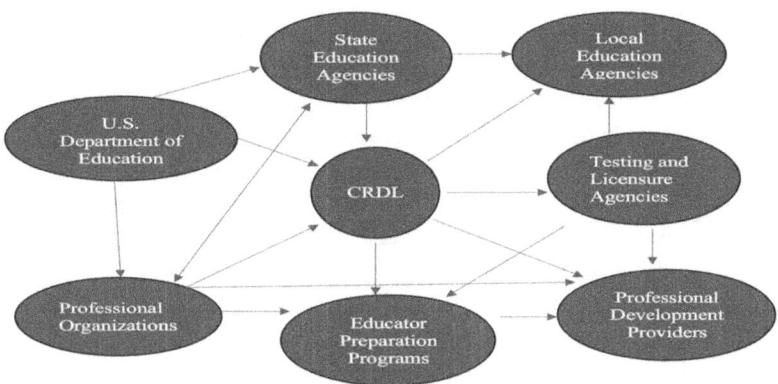

Figure 6.1. Systems mapping for implementing CRDL in education

U.S. Department of Education

The U.S. Department of Education sets policy about the importance of topics. Related to data and evidence use, more than two decades ago, the department established the Institute of Education Sciences (IES) with an emphasis on using hard evidence. The Statewide Longitudinal Data Systems (SLDS) Grant Program was established and funded several rounds of grants to help states develop the technological infrastructure to support data use. The SLDSs are a major conduit along the EDFacts data highway that communicates data from local to state education agencies up to the federal level. Much of these data are for compliance and accountability purposes. They are to meet federal reporting requirements. According to the SLDS Program (n.d.), "the SLDSs should help states, districts, schools, educators, and other stakeholders to make data-informed decisions to improve student learning and outcomes; as well as to facilitate research to increase student achievement and close achievement gaps." Given the investment, it is safe to assume that the department wants educators to use data, but the educators must have the skills to do so.

The department has provided funding to create state-level data technology infrastructures. It has also provided a vision for data use directly through policy statements by high-level officials and indirectly through funding streams and publications. Various secretaries of education have provided their views of data use. For example, Margaret Spellings firmly came down on the side of data for accountability whereas Arne Duncan promoted data for continuous improvement. Such messaging resonates to states and districts about what the department deems important.

In terms of publications, one of the earliest IES practice guides pertained to data-driven decision making, but its focus was on linking data use to student achievement (Hamilton et al., 2009). The five recommendations culled from existing research remain salient in the data literature. Much research and development, stimulated by the recommendations, has been conducted since the practice guide was published, and those recommendation still apply.

Support for culturally responsive practices remains more limited. The regional educational laboratories, funded through the department, have addressed the topic through blogs (Goldstein, 2017, 2020; Nishoka, 2021), Ask a REL (Regional Educational Lab) questions, other resources such as infographics (REL Midwest, n.d.; REL Southwest, 2021), and webinars (Mandinach et al., 2019) as a response to each REL's regional needs.

The most directly relevant publication is a forum guide to data literacy (NFES, 2024) as noted in chapter 3. The National Forum on Education Statistics (n.d.) produces guides and resources on various topics that affect schools, districts, and state agencies around the use of data and statistics. The guides are informed by research and best practices and contain relevant case studies. As one of the authors representing REL West, I ensured that data literacy for teachers (DLFT) and CRDL were represented. This publication should be a useful resource for all educators.

Despite the department's focus on data, what has not happened is a concerted effort to provide funds for capacity building through professional development and research. Funding for research through IES requires student achievement to be an outcome measure. This limits the kinds of research projects that are fundable because the logic models do not readily support linking culturally responsive practices or data use directly to student performance. What is more pressing, in my opinion, is funding for capacity building around CRDL. If the department were to fund capacity building, for example, through the Comprehensive Center program, the RELs, or other funding programs, that would be a significant statement about the importance of the topic. Funding indicates a level of criticality that goes beyond vision statements made by leaders who come and go with different administrations and different agendas. Explicit vision statements do matter, but funding is more lasting as would be accepting proposals for research and development on CRDL, the whole child, and equity.

Because of the emphasis on local control of education, the relationship between the federal and state levels can be complex. Policy statements can make a difference in determining the importance of topics such as CRDL. But as we have seen, some states have made their own policies, sometimes diametrically opposite to the federal ones. These topics are often highly politicized and contentious, but they do impact what is taught and how topics are taught. CRDL might well be one of those topics that becomes politicized.

State Education Agencies

State education agencies play a crucial role in determining the skill sets educators must have to practice in their state. They develop standards for credentialing that the states' educator preparation programs must follow. These standards likely impact the curricula by providing messaging about what skills and knowledge the agency requires of the educators. Agencies may also have codes of ethics. Thus, explicit messaging around the content of the standards and codes provides guidelines to educator preparation and to local education agencies about what the state deems important. As noted in chapter 3, some states have done a better job of addressing data literacy and culturally responsive practices than others (Mandinach et al., 2015; Mandinach et al., 2017; Muniz, 2019). States that have adopted the InTASC standards can be considered more aligned to CRDL, but likely the attention to the construct is unconscious or a by-product of the adoption. The more explicit the standards in terms of data literacy and culturally responsive practices, the easier it is to translate the standards into program curricula. Therefore, it is important to communicate explicitly to state representatives the meaning of CRDL (Mandinach & Warner, 2022) so that the skill set can be incorporated into state standards.

State agencies serve as the conduit from districts to the U.S. Department of Education. Much of the data that pass along the data highway are for accountability and compliance, but the messaging and vision from a chief state school officer can be important and impact the state's educators. This book was written at a time when states have widely different perspectives on which topics are valued and which topics are considered less desirable or even banned. For example, Arizona's current (as of 2023–2024) superintendent of public instruction ran on a platform to ban critical race theory. The politicization of education content may well work against the culturally responsive component of CRDL while promoting the use of data more for accountability than for continuous improvement and an equity lens. Messaging from state education agencies makes a difference. It has a direct effect on the state's schools, districts, and educators.

Local Education Agencies

Schools and districts are at the heart of implementing CRDL practices. Leadership must provide the resources to create a vision and a culture for appropriate data use, messaging about using an equity lens and addressing the needs of all students, rather than marginalizing students by solely using accountability data. That said, districts still must provide accountability data to the state agencies and are held accountable. They must adhere to state policies and standards. But in the end, districts are still responsible for educating all children in the most effective and appropriate manner possible.

Districts interface with educator preparation programs that sometimes provide teacher candidates for their practical experiences and supply new graduates. Districts should work with the programs to ensure that candidates and graduates have the necessary skill set while also creating an environment, such as a strong data culture, that can sustain the implementation of CRDL in practice. Sometimes there is a disconnect. Students are prepared to use data in their programs but are hired by a district without a data culture, data teams, or coaches, and their skills seem misaligned. Or the converse: candidates are not prepared, and they enter a district where data use is expected.

Districts also interact with professional development providers. The issue for CRDL, or data literacy and culturally responsive practices more generally, is prioritization; topics may not rise to the top of the list in terms of the expenditure of limited training funds. It is important for districts to support, encourage, and expect their educators to know how to use data effectively and responsibly to meet the needs of all students. An explicit vision for data use is critical, but even more so, district leadership must devote the resources that help build the human capacity.

Professional Organizations

Professional organizations are essential to communicating the importance of educator skills and knowledge. Several organizations play key roles: the National Association of State Directors of Teacher Education and Certification (NASDTEC); the American Association of Colleges for Teacher Education (AACTE); the Council for the Accreditation of Educator Preparation (CAEP); the Association of Teacher Educators (ATE); the National Association of Secondary School Principals (NASSP); and the Council of Chief State School Officers (CCSSO).

Many of these organizations produce standards and guidelines for educator preparation. Perhaps most relevant are the InTASC Standards produced by CCSSO (2013). As noted in chapter 3, this document contains ten standards from which can be extracted many skills, knowledge, and dispositions that are relevant to CRDL (Mandinach et al., 2015; Mandinach et al., 2017; Muniz, 2019). CCSSO (2012) issued policy papers about the importance of topics such as data use. Also relevant is the *Model Code of Ethics for Educators* (MCEE) developed by NASDTEC (2023). As noted in chapter 3, until 2022 the MCEE failed to address data use, at which point the code introduced a principle about the responsible use of data. The MCEE also includes a principle about "Responsibility to Students" that addresses cultural sensitivity. CAEP and AACTE have promoted DLFT in various ways, most prominently through a keynote speech at its national conference (Mandinach & Gummer, 2016a). At that time, a survey was administered to conference attendees to ask about the importance of DLFT. Overwhelmingly, the respondents reported that they believe data literacy should be taught in educator preparation and it should be integrated into the curricula (Mandinach & Nunnaley, 2017). Other organizations, such as ATE, provide workshops on materials and resources that can be introduced into teacher preparation.

These agencies can bring awareness to policies, provide guidance to educator preparation programs about topics that should be covered in their curricula, and disseminate resources. These professional organizations can work with state education agencies to ensure that topics such as CRDL are embedded in state standards. They can communicate the importance of the concept in their conferences to bring awareness of CRDL to their members and stakeholders. They can communicate the need for CRDL to be included in licensure and credentialing, which also can impact the testing agencies.

Educator Preparation Programs

Educator preparation programs are one of the most essential elements in the system to effect change and help create an educator workforce that can implement CRDL. Programs provide the essential knowledge and skills for educators in their initial preparation and through further reinforcement in graduate courses. The programs are caught in the middle of a complex, interactive system. They must adhere to state requirements and professional organizations in terms of standards to which their curricula should be aligned. They strive to produce graduates who can pass the credentialing and licensure tests. The programs provide candidates and graduates to districts so they must be responsive to their needs, especially institutions that serve specific regions.

Aside from the related stakeholders, the programs have their own challenges in terms of adopting CRDL into their curricula. First, they must be aware of the construct. Second, they must perceive the need for their students to acquire CRDL skills. By necessity, some universities with a focus on underserved populations may be more likely to have introduced courses on culturally responsive practices. Third, programs are overwhelmed with requirements, so adding yet another one may be difficult. And even with the need, a question remains whether faculty are able and willing to integrate the principles of CRDL into their courses. The scenarios found in chapters 4 and 5 can help to provide much needed resources for instructors and professors, but can they find places in their courses and are they capable of using them effectively? There likely is a need for capacity building at that level as well. These challenges are part of the rationale for making the scenarios user-friendly, flexible, and easy to integrate.

Professional Development Providers

Professional development providers must be responsive to the needs of schools and districts. They provide technical assistance and in-service training. The providers are guided, to a small extent, by the standards laid out by the professional organizations and the state credentialing agencies. They extend the trajectory of educator learning past their formal course work in educator preparation programs.

In examining the content of data-related professional development conducted to launch the data literacy work, Mandinach and Gummer (2011) found many of the mainstream providers, books, and resources only peripherally addressed the 50 plus skills and knowledge identified as part of DLFT. Generic professional development most certainly fails to address data literacy. Mandinach and Nunnaley (2021) reviewed the main data-related professional development programs to see how the topic of data ethics is addressed. Even the two most popular programs, Using Data (Love et al., 2008) and Data Wise (Boudett et al., 2013) tangentially cover the topic, although equity is an underlying theme in Using Data. One of the clear recommendations from that examination was for both data-related and generic professional development to include or integrate data ethics into their materials as educators must understand about appropriate and inappropriate data use across their practice. Similar comments can be made about the integration of the concepts of culturally responsive teaching. The inclusion may be subsumed within examples so that users at least are introduced to the concept.

The identified need is for the development of materials and resources around CRDL that can be adopted by professional development providers in the easiest, most flexible manner. The scenarios in this volume serve as a first step in addressing that need. Additional materials can be developed that may be specific to different contexts, districts, and locales. Therefore, it is important for the development process to collaborate with the providers and the districts to better meet their needs around CRDL by building awareness of the need and importance and by providing readily usable materials that can be parts of trainings, stand alone, or for individual use.

Testing Organizations and Licensure Agencies

Testing organizations require educators to demonstrate their knowledge of content, methods, and other topics for the purpose of certification and licensure. Educational Testing Service (2015a, 2015b) has assessments, some performance-based and others written, such as the PRAXIS tests and NOTE. The edTPA (SCALE, 2014) is a performance-based activity with rubrics against which candidates are measured. The content of these assessments and the underlying knowledge and skills required of them should be aligned to state standards, educator preparation programs, and the emerging needs of schools and districts.

From a systems perspective, there are complex relationships. Standards should influence the content of the assessments and the content of educator preparation programs' curricula. Yet the content of the assessments may also influence the curricula (i.e., what is tested gets taught). Conversely, the curricula may inform the assessments. Educator preparation programs can be evaluated on the percentage of their students that succeed on the assessments and receive their credentials and licenses. Therefore, it is incumbent on the programs to ensure an alignment to the tests.

In terms of CRDL, what is needed is to build awareness with the testing organizations about both data literacy and culturally responsive practices. The testing organizations then can begin to introduce and integrate the concepts into their assessments in an informed manner. Attempts were made to do this around DLFT (Mandinach, 2017) at Educational Testing Service.

CONCLUDING COMMENTS

As you can see from the interactions depicted in figure 6.1 and the descriptions of the stakeholder groups, clearly there are complex interactions that can foment or impede change. Each stakeholder group has unique responsibilities and interests. However, their interactions with other groups are essential and exert various types of pressures and leverage points. Each of these agencies must act and be willing to incorporate CRDL. They must perceive the need to do so. The agencies must become aware of the importance of CRDL in educational practice, embrace the construct, and then effect change within their agency and across others. Resistance is natural, and challenges are abundant. But quoting the lead penguin in the *Madagascar* movie, "Don't give me excuses; give me results." Or, paraphrasing, "Don't bring me problems; bring me solutions." The problem is recognizable and complex. Students are more diverse, requiring diverse data sources to help educators make informed decisions. The data sources range far beyond student performance indices. And the data must be used in ways that do not marginalize any group of students but, instead, invoke an equity lens and assume a whole child perspective. Educators must acquire this skill set, but they cannot do it on their own. Each of the stakeholder groups discussed here has an essential role to play in ensuring that current and future educators understand the importance of CRDL and can implement the construct in their practice.

The problem or issue is recognizable. What would be the solution? Here are a few actionable steps to take based on this discussion:

- Build awareness.
- Provide a concrete, explicit definition of CRDL (we have a well-developed definition, but it must be broadly disseminated, acknowledged, and implemented).
- Work with the stakeholder groups, particularly the state standards staff, professional organizations, and educator preparation programs.
- Develop and provide user-friendly materials and resources to educator preparation programs, professional development providers, and educators.
- Sustain this trajectory to reinforce the construct and update CRDL as needed.

Chapter 7

What Needs to Happen

ACTIONABLE NEXT STEPS

I will wrap up the discussion of CRDL with a challenge to the education field. I lay out the complexities that create challenges to effect change. These are realities that all educators are facing. I conclude with a set of recommendations that are concrete actions steps that can be taken to stimulate the enculturation of CRDL into educational practice.

COMPLEXITIES

Before considering the actions steps that need to occur to ensure that CRDL becomes an essential part of educational practice, some important caveats must be stated. First, data use is not a panacea. It is not the solution to all of education's problems. But data use done effectively and responsibly can help to inform practice in important ways, based on evidence rather than anecdotes or gut feelings. It can provide educators with hard evidence and indicators of issues, questions, student strengths and weaknesses, and directions for actionable steps.

Second, data use is not easy. I have laid out the many skills, knowledge, and dispositions that educators should have to be considered data literate and to use CRDL. However, the actionable component has always been the conundrum in DLFT and is now even more challenging having added the culturally responsive component. Educators may know their content and their methods, but the original issue that has persisted is how to transform the data into actionable steps based on the specific content—that is, the pedagogical content knowledge, or what I referred to as pedagogical data literacy.

Now add the component of cultural responsiveness that includes using an asset model, an equity lens, and a whole child approach. It adds another set of complexities about which educators must be aware. In the data field, the guidance was only to use data that are actionable. Now the thinking has changed. The CR component of CRDL adds the complexity of student context as a major emphasis in trying to gain a comprehensive understanding of the student to enable actionable steps that incorporate the whole child. It shifts the focus from a deficit model to an asset model that requires modifying communications, such as learner weaknesses or problems of practice. More importantly, the CR component requires several consequential shifts. Educators must consider the diversity of their students, move away from confirmation bias, confront their own biases, and assume an equity mind-set. These are challenges.

Educators are not expected to be able to act on issues beyond their classroom. But knowing the context certainly can help to provide a broader, more informative understanding of the student.

A third complexity goes to the heart of data-driven decision making. Mandinach and Gummer (2021) talk about data ethics in terms of using the "appropriate" data and the "appropriate" methods to inform "sound" interpretations. Having valid data no doubt is essential. Hobor and Marwell (2022) caution that users must be mindful of the limitations of data as well as the analytic methods. As noted in chapter 2, data must be timely, accurate, relevant, and aligned to the question at hand. Similarly, the analytics and the skills of DLFT are needed. The American Statistical Association (2022) describes in its code of ethics the need to use appropriate methods to examine data. The same is true in education. The conundrum for me, and something I have heard repeatedly in my work, is how to determine whether the interpretations are solid, valid, and appropriate. Cronbach (1988) described that validity is not just a property of an assessment but also of the interpretations made from the results of an assessment. The same is true here. But how do we know whether an interpretation is valid and appropriate? Adding to the complexity, Gaddy and Scott (2020) note that "data are not neutral" and that there are "silent factors that reflect the interests, assumptions, and biases" of the data users (p. 1).

I provide a personal example to highlight the complexity. In 2019, I injured my leg in a bicycle accident. After a trip to Hawaii, I returned with a large necrotic wound on my lower leg. After a seeing the primary care doctor and then going to the emergency room, I was admitted to the hospital for four days. The initial doctor's visit yielded a bandage and some antibiotics. He asked if I needed an X-ray. I knew I did not have anything broken. The emergency room examined me and immediately admitted me. Over the course of my stay, several doctors examined the wound. Every doctor had a different diagnosis and a course of recommended treatment based on their perspective and specialty. Each of them was presented with the same data, but their interpretations and suggested actionable steps differed. The infectious disease specialist said one thing, the hospitalist another, and the wound doctor, yet something else.

As an individual who understands data-driven decision making, I found the situation interesting. As a patient, unfortunately I found the situation problematic in terms of which interpretation and subsequent action steps were preferred. I made a choice that apparently angered the wound care specialist, who later asked me why he should help me, given that my decision was contrary to his recommended course of action. He was rather unprofessional. The point here is that the same data can be seen through differing lenses based on experience, expertise, and even bias. Therein lies the conundrum.

Let us use this example and extrapolate to education. In education, there might not be several experts from differing fields looking at the same data and then deciding. There might be a data team or grade-level team that collaboratively examines the same data and then provides individual perspectives. The perspectives might differ. Hopefully, there would be collaborative, cooperative discussions about what the data mean and what possible actions might be taken based on those data. Although the IES practice guide on data use recommends that students become their own data-driven decision makers (Hamilton et al., 2009), the instructional, behavioral, or other decision ultimately falls to the educators. In addition, the question of whether the action steps "worked" is ambiguous and problematic. In the medical example, one could define "working" as that my leg wound healed. One could ask whether the decision was the right one or the best one—that is, might the wound have healed faster or better, given some other treatment. In education, the definitions are not so clear cut. What does "work" mean? Is the student making progress or something else? The term is contextual and is not a one-size-fits-all solution. Every student is different and brings unique characteristics to the classroom. Additional questions about "work" might be for whom? under what circumstances?

and with what context in mind? One might also want to know why so that the explanation can also be a learning opportunity for the educator. What is it that I did right to help this student from which I can learn?

RECOMMENDED STEPS

As was noted in chapter 6, the change process to ensure that CRDL becomes embedded in educational practice is systemic and complex. Some recommendations were touched on in the prior chapter because of the systemic nature of the change process. It will require a multistep process with buy-in from many stakeholder groups.

Build Awareness and Promote the Importance of CRDL

The first step toward the broad use of CRDL is to build awareness of the construct and to promote its importance to a wide variety of stakeholder groups. Many people are confused about data literacy, confounding it with assessment literacy, as discussed earlier in the book. It is important to differentiate the two constructs and make a case for a broad view of data. The hurdle here is to help people understand that that data are more than test scores, and educators must know how to use a broad range of diverse data. This means dispelling a long-held belief about what data are.

Building a case for the CR of CRDL may well be a challenging enterprise in some states, especially where topics such as critical race theory and LGBTQ issues are eschewed. Thus, it is even more important to clearly communicate to stakeholders, especially high-level policy makers why CRDL is important to understand the whole child and how the construct can positively impact all students through effective, responsive data use. Finally, part of the process of building awareness is to shift the conversation about data use away from data for accountability and from shaming and blaming. It is important for stakeholders to understand how diverse data sources for the purpose of continuous improvement for students, classes, schools, and districts can positively impact and inform the education process.

Engage Professional Organizations

It is essential to engage professional organizations that are impactful in terms of requisite educator skills and knowledge. Some key professional organizations can influence their members about CRDL. Perhaps the most influential is NASDTEC, whose members represent state education agencies and standards commissions. Bringing awareness to the individuals who are responsible for state standards can be an important leverage point. A second organization is the American Association of Colleges for Teacher Education (AACTE), a member organization that includes hundreds of educator preparation programs. If AACTE promotes the importance of CRDL to its members, the programs might be more likely to embed CRDL in their curricula. Similarly, the Council for the Accreditation of Educator Preparation (CAEP) promotes standards for the accreditation of educator preparation. Both CAEP and AACTE recognized the importance of DLFT by having the topic as the keynote address at one of their annual conferences (Mandinach & Gummer, 2016a). That keynote reached nearly 2,000 attendees, building awareness of the construct and making a case for its importance in educator preparation. The Association of Teacher Educators (ATE) is a member organization that has broad networks nationally and regionally to provide information to instructors and professors of teacher education. These individuals are on the frontline of providing quality instruction in teacher education and through clinical practice. Building awareness and providing resources to members of ATE can stimulate broad dissemination of CRDL. Finally, and at a different level of engagement, is the Council of Chief State School Offices (CCSSO). Bringing awareness to the highest level of education leadership can help to create an understanding of the construct, which then could lead to policy statements and changes to standards within and across states.

Embed CRDL in State and Professional Standards

Following from the prior recommendation, it is important to have CRDL reflected in state and professional standards. Given that a common definition of CRDL exists and key skills have been identified, it would be possible for all or part of the construct to be written into the standards. Like DLFT, having at minimum key skills and knowledge embedded in the standards would be a first step. For the states that have a stand-alone data literacy standard, have that standard modified to reflect CRDL, not just data literacy. Having CRDL in the standards is a direct message to educator preparation programs that CRDL's skills and knowledge should and must be part of educators' repertoire.

Collaborate With State Education Agencies

State education agencies create policies and requirements about the skills and knowledge educators must have to practice in their states. They create standards and codes of ethics. They work with their educator preparation programs to communicate important skills that are expected of graduates. The policies and requirements resonate through the programs and to schools and districts. For example, North Carolina developed a statement about educators and data literacy (Mandinach et al., 2015). Arizona worked with its educator preparation programs to create a rubric to be completed about how their curricula were addressing data literacy. Washington and Alaska have stand-alone standards on CRT.

Embed CRDL in Licensing and Credentialing

Following the prior recommendations, ensuring that CRDL is reflected in licensing and credentialing will make a strong statement about the importance of the construct. In this way, educators must be able to demonstrate CRDL skills and knowledge as part of their licensure process.

Collaborate With Local Education Agencies

Schools and districts are on the frontlines in educational practice. They must be aware of the need for their educators to use CRDL skills and knowledge and to help them obtain the needed training. They must require that newly hired educators have CRDL skills, coming from their preparation programs or from other districts. They must create a culture of expectation for effective, responsible data use, including data teams, data coaches, technologies, and the expectations for using an asset model, equity lens, and a whole child perspective. Leadership must lay out an explicit vision and communicate it directly to their educators. The agencies can work with educator preparation programs to help fulfill staffing needs with the requisite skill set. They can look to their state agencies for guidance. They also must look to the communities they serve to ensure that they are addressing the needs of all children through using CRDL.

Work With Educator Preparation Programs

Educator preparation programs, both at the graduate and undergraduate level, are one of the key players in the complex system of change. An important step in embedding CRDL into educator practice is to have the construct introduced in preservice programs and then reinforced in graduate programs and in practice. The survey administered at the 2016 CAEP conference (Mandinach & Nunnaley, 2017) showed that almost every attendee thought that teaching data literacy was essential. The results further showed that respondents preferred an integrated approach rather than stand-alone data courses. They recognized that curricula are already full and complex, so adding another course would not be pragmatic or realistic. Instead, they thought that integrating data literacy into existing courses was the best strategy. Generalizing from these findings, the same could be said for CRDL. Integration and providing materials that professors and instructors can flexibly and easily embed in their courses would mitigate the issues of who could teach a course and how it would become part of the curricula. Thus, an essential recommendation is to work closely with educator preparation programs to help them use existing CRDL materials and perhaps codevelop other materials as the needs emerge.

Work With Professional Development Providers

Professional development providers have outreach to the many schools and districts across the country. They can be the conduit for CRDL to the existing cohort of educators to provide the needed training and resources to help build their CRDL. A major challenge here continues to be limited funds and prioritizing existing funds to what likely is considered more critical expenditures of monies. CRDL is unlikely to rise to the top as more pressing topics may instead receive funds and attention. However, one strategy here is to find ways for CRDL to be embedded in generic professional development and technical assistance, not just data-related or culturally responsive ones. For current data providers, it is important to ensure that they incorporate the broader range of data and focus on the tenets of culturally responsive practices. For culturally responsive practices providers, the reverse is applicable; ensure that those providers incorporate the tenets of data literacy.

Develop Materials

The scenarios in chapters 4 and 5 are a first step toward developing materials that can teach about CRDL. Much more development can and should be undertaken. As the construct becomes more engrained in educational practice, more and different uses will emerge that can stimulate development of new forms of resources through different media and technologies. Perhaps this is a challenge to the field about how to create new materials and resources for CRDL that can better engage educators in implementing the skills, knowledge, and dispositions beyond what is presented in this volume.

Stimulate a Mind-Set Change

An essential stimulus to embedding CRDL in educational practice is a fundamental mind-set change that begins with acknowledging the need to use data effectively and responsibly, highlighting the importance of using an asset model, an equity lens, and a whole child perspective. It also requires the philosophical transition from data for accountability to data for continuous improvement. It moves the data discussion from a mechanistic approach to test scores to a humanistic understanding of students. In chapter 1, I note the need for a paradigm shift in data use. This shift requires educators to undergo a fundamental change in mind-set.

As Frameworks (2020) notes, shifting mind-sets involves several key elements.

- First, stakeholders must recognize the potential benefits of a change.
- Second, seeing success early in the change process can stimulate further progress.
- Third, recognize that external factors can impact the change process.
- Fourth, the intended shift must be realistic and relevant.
- Fifth, it is essential to acknowledge that change takes time.

To this point, I use an old lightbulb joke. How many psychologists does it take to change a lightbulb? The answer is one, but the lightbulb must want to change. Education is a complex system with many moving components and often opposing pressures. Recognition that educators should and must address the needs of all children is essential but highly complex. Educators must address the long-term goals, not just the easy, short-term wins. This perspective requires a fundamental mind-set shift.

A CLOSING THOUGHT

The Arizona Speakers Series brings in prominent individuals to speak on diverse and important topics. Here are timely comments by three of the speakers that are relevant to CRDL.

First, Stacey Abrams (2023) discussed that people need to move beyond beliefs to information, facts, and evidence. She used the term *ipse dixit*, meaning that people must avoid making assertions or holding opinions without credible evidence and being based in facts. Although she was speaking in generalities, this premise certainly pertains to educational practice. Abrams described her vision for society, in general, that can be translated to education: be curious, solve problems, and do good. Educators should be challenged to attain all three parts of her vision.

Second, Anderson Cooper (2022) was asked how CNN verifies sources for accuracy before releasing a story. He commented that CNN uses three series of vetting and sometimes things still fall through the cracks, but their process of fact-checking is rigorous. This is important to data use in many ways. Accuracy is essential or all sorts of false interpretations might result.

Third, at the conclusion of each session, the speaker is asked about what they are most optimistic. Former President Obama (2021) was a speaker earlier in the same season with Cooper. His response is a perfect coda to this volume. Paraphrasing, he said that we can be optimistic about the future if educators help children to understand fact from fiction and learn how to use data and evidence. Further, the country would be in a better place if everyone knew how to do that. This was said at a time when misinformation and disinformation were rampant. Let us take President Obama's comment as a call to action. Let us put in place a deep understanding of and appreciation for how to use data effectively and appropriately. This should be the responsibility of all educators and all citizens.

References

Abrams, S. (2023, October 11). Arizona Speakers Series [speech transcript]. https://arizonaspeakersseries.com/

American Statistical Association. (2022). Ethical guidelines for statistical practice. Committee on Professional Ethics of the American Statistical Association. https://www.amstat.org/docs/default-source/amstat-documents/ethicalguidelines.pdf?Status=Master&sfvrsn=bdeeafdd_6/

Argyris, C., & Schon, D. A. (1974). *Theory in Practice: Increasing Professional Effectiveness*. Jossey-Bass.

Au, W. (2007). High-stakes testing and curricular control: A qualitative metasynthesis. *Educational Researcher, 35*(5), 258–267.

Bambrick-Santoyo, P. (2010). *Driven by Data: A Practical Guide to Improve Instruction*. Jossey-Bass.

Barat, V. X., et al. (2021, October). *Chronic absenteeism in Arizona: A description of K–8 trends 2017–2021*. https://www.helios.org/media/zeckn0xp/brief-az-chronic-absence-report_final-draft_with-appendix_proofed.pdf

Barat, V. X. et al. (2022, July). *Missing too much school: Trends in K–8 chronic absenteeism in Arizona during the pandemic*. https://helios.org/media/hzydjckw/22hls024-az-chronic-absence-brief_final_digital.pdf

Beck, J. S. (2020). "Speak truth to power ourselves": Teaching social justice in a teacher residency program. *Teacher Education Quarterly, 47*(3), 75–95.

Beck, J. S., Morgan, J. J., & Whitesides, H. (2019, April). *Providing construct coherence between assessment and data literacy: A systematic review of the literature*. Paper presented at the annual conference of the American Educational Research Association, Toronto.

Berliner, D. C. (2011). Rational responses to high stakes testing: The case of curriculum narrowing and the harm that follows. *Cambridge Journal of Education, 41*(3), 287–302.

Bernhardt, V. L. (2004). *Data Analysis for Continuous School Improvement* (2nd ed.). Eye on Education.

Bertrand, M., & Marsh, J. A. (2015). Teachers' sensemaking of data and implications for equity. *American Educational Research Journal, 52*(5), 861–93.

Bertrand, M., & Marsh, J. A. (2021). How data-driven reform can drive deficit thinking. *Kappan, 102*, 35–39.

Biden, J. (2016, April). *Operation Educate the Educators: Recognizing and supporting military-connected students through university-based research, community partnerships, and teacher education programs* [Speech transcript]. Annual conference of the American Educational Research Association, Washington, DC.

Booher-Jennings, J. (2005). "Educational triage" and the Texas accountability system. *American Educational Research Journal, 42*(2), 231–268.

Boudett, K. P., City, E. A., & Murnane, R. J. (Eds.). (2005). *Data Wise: A Step-by-Step Guide to Using Assessment Results to Improve Teaching and Learning*. Harvard Education Press.

Boudett, K. P., City, E. A., & Murnane, R. J. (Eds.). (2013). *Data Wise: A Step-by-Step Guide to Using Assessment Results to Improve Teaching and Learning, Revised and Expanded Edition.* Harvard Education Press.

Braaten, M., Bradford, C., Kirchgasler, K. L., & Fox Barocas, S. (2017). How data use for accountability undermines equitable science education. *Journal of Educational Administration, 55*(4), 427–446.

Branch Alliance. (2021). *A primer on inclusive instruction.* https://resources.educatordiversity.org/?query=Inclusive+instruction

Connecticut State Department of Education. (n.d.). *Creating a culturally sustaining classroom through building relationships and intentional instructional practices.* https://portal.ct.gov/sde/-/media/SDE/NetStat/NetStat_5_14_21/Relationships_Culturally_Sustaining_Classrooms.pdf

Cooper, A. (2022, February 25). Arizona Speakers Series [speech transcript]. https://arizonaspeakersseries.com/

Corno, L. (2008). On teaching adaptively. *Educational Psychologist, 43*(3), 161–173.

Cronbach, L. J., & Snow, R. E. (1977). *Aptitudes and Instructional Methods: A Handbook for Research on Interactions.* Irvington.

Council of Chief State School Officers. (2012). *Our responsibility, our promise: Transforming educator preparation and entry into the profession.* https://ccsso.org/sites/default/files/2017-10/Our%20Responsibility%20Our%20Promise_2012.pdf

Council of Chief State School Officers. (2013). *InTASC Model Core Teaching Standards and Learning Progressions for Teachers* 1.0. Interstate Teacher Assessment and Support Consortium. https://ccsso.org/sites/default/files/2017-12/2013_INTASC_Learning_Progressions_for_Teachers.pdf

Data Quality Campaign. (2014). *Teacher data literacy: It's about time.* https://dataqualitycampaign.org/wp-content/uploads/2016/03/DQC-Data-Literacy-Brief.pdf

Datnow, A. (2017). *Opening or closing doors for students? Equity and data-driven decision-making.* https://research.acer.edu.au/cgi/viewcontent.cgi?article=1317&context=research_conference

Datnow, A., Greene, J. C., & Gannon-Slater, N. (2017). Data use for equity: Implications for teaching, leadership, and policy. *Journal of Educational Administration, 55*(4), 354–360.

Datnow, A., & Hubbard, L. (2016). Teacher capacity for and beliefs about data-driven decision making: A literature review of international research. *Journal of Educational Change, 17*(1), 7–28.

Datnow, A., & Park, V. (2018). Opening or closing doors for students? Equity and data use in schools. *Journal of Educational Change, 19*(2), 131–152.

Diamond, J. B., & Cooper, K. (2007). The uses of testing data in urban elementary schools: Some lessons from Chicago. *Yearbook of the National Society for the Study of Education, 106*(1), 241–263.

Diamond, J. B., & Spillane, J. P. (2004). High-stakes accountability in urban elementary schools: Challenge or reproducing inequality? *Teachers College Record, 106*, 1145–1176.

Dictionary.com (n.d.). *Allyship.* https://www.dictionary.com/browse/allyship

Dodman, S. L., Swalwell, K., DeMulder, E. K., View, J. L., & Stribling, S. M. (2021). Critical data-driven decision making: A conceptual model of data use for equity. *Teaching and Teacher Education, 99*, 1–11.

Dover, A. G. (2013). Teaching for social justice: From conceptual frameworks to classroom practices. *Multicultural Perspectives, 15*(1), 3–11.

Dover, A. G. (2015). "Promoting acceptance" or "preparing warrior scholars": Variance in teaching for social justice vision and praxis. *Equity & Excellence in Education, 48*(3), 361–372.

Educational Testing Service. (2015a). *National Observational Teacher Examination.* www.ets.org/note

Educational Testing Service. (2015b). *Praxis.* www.ets.org.praxis

Equitable Data Working Group. (2022, April). *A vision for equitable data: Recommendations from the Equitable Data Working Group.* https://www.whitehouse.gov/wp-content/uploads/2022/04/eo13985-vision-for-equitable-data.pdf

Equitable Data Working Group. (2023, April). *Progress on the implementation of the recommendations of the Equitable Data Working Group.* https://www.whitehouse.gov/wp-content/uploads/2023/03/Progress-on-Equitable-Data-Mar2023.pdf

Frameworks. (2020, June). *Mindset Shifts: What are they? Why do they matter? How do they happen?* https://www.frameworksinstitute.org/wp-content/uploads/2021/02/FRAJ8064-Mindset-Shifts-200612-WEB.pdf

Gaddy, M., & Scott, K. (2020, June). *Principles for advancing equitable data practice.* https://www.urban.org/sites/default/files/publication/102346/principles-for-advancing-equitable-data-practice_0.pdf

Gannon-Slater, N., La Londe, P. G., Crenshaw, H. L., Evans, M. E., Greene, J. E., & Schwandt, T. A. (2017). Advancing equity in accountability and organizational cultures of data use. *Journal of Educational Administration, 55*(4), 361–375.

Garner, B., Thorne, J. K., & Horn, I. S. Teachers interpreting data for instructional decisions: Where does equity come in? *Journal of Educational Administration, 55*(4), 407–426.

Gay, G. (2002). Preparing for culturally responsive teaching. *Journal of Teacher Education, 53*, 106–116.

Gay, G. (2018). *Culturally Responsive Teaching: Theory, Research, and Practice* (3rd ed.). Teachers College Press.

Goldstein, C. (2017, September). *Culturally responsive instruction: Best practices and supports.* REL Midwest. https://ies.ed.gov/ncee/rel/Products/Region/midwest/Blog/10146

Goldstein, C. (2020, October). *Resource roundup: Culturally responsive practices.* REL Midwest. https://ies.ed.gov/ncee/rel/Products/Region/midwest/Blog/10019

Gorski, P. C. (2016). Equity literacy: More than celebrating diversity. *Diversity in Education, 11*(1) (Spring), 12–14.

Gorski, P. C., & Pothini, S. G. (2018). *Case Studies on Diversity and Social Justice Education* (2nd ed.). Routledge.

Gummer, E. S., & Mandinach, E. B. (2015). Building a conceptual framework for data literacy. *Teachers College Record, 117*(4), 1–22. http://www.tcrecord.org/PrintContent.asp?ContentID=17856

Hamilton, L., Halverson, R., Jackson, S., Mandinach, E., Supovitz, J., & Wayman, J. (2009). *Using student achievement data to support instructional decision making* (NCEE 2009-4067). National Center for Education Evaluation and Regional Assistance, Institute of Education Sciences, U.S. Department of Education. https://ies.ed.gov/ncee/wwc/Docs/PracticeGuide/dddm_pg_092909

Hargreaves, A., & Braun, H. (2013). *Data-driven improvement and accountability.* University of Colorado, National Education Policy Center. https://nepc.colorado.edu/publication/data-driven-improvement-accountability

Hobor, G., & Marwell, N. (2022, October). *What can we do about biases baked into data?* https://www.rwjf.org/en/insights/blog/2022/10/what-can-we-do-about-biases-baked-into-data.html

Hoover, N. R., & Abrams, L. M. (2013). Teachers' instructional use of summative student assessment data. *Applied Measurement in Education, 26*(3), 219–231.

Khalifa, M. A., Gooden, M. A., & Davis, J. E. (2016). Culturally responsive school leadership: A synthesis of the literature. *Review of Educational Research, 86*(4), 1272–1311.

Kunichoff, Y. (2023a, March). State school superintendent starts hotline for public to report "inappropriate" lessons. *Arizona Republic.* https://www.azcentral.com/story/news/local/arizona-education/2023/03/08/state-schools-chief-tom-horne-opens-hotline-for-inappropriate-lessons/69985559007/

Kunichoff, Y. (2023b, June). Robocalls flood hotline for school complains. *Arizona Republic.* https://www.azcentral.com/story/news/local/arizona-education/2023/06/05/most-calls-to-tom-horne-arizona-hotline-to-report-inappropriate-lessons-are-pranks/70283441007/

Ladson-Billings, G. (1995). Toward a theory of culturally relevant pedagogy. *American Educational Research Journal, 32*(3), 465–491.

Lasater, K., Bengston, E., & Albiladi, W. S. (2021). Data use for equity?: How data practices incite deficit thinking in schools. *Studies in Educational Evaluation, 69*, 1–10.

Love, N., Stiles, K. E., Mundry, S. E., & DiRanna, K. (2008). *The Data Coach's Guide to Improving Learning for All Students: Unleashing the Power of Collaborative Inquiry.* Corwin.

Macdonald-Evoy, J. (2022, January). GOP bill would force teaches to out LGBTQ students to parents. *AZ Mirror.* https://www.azmirror.com/2022/01/26/gop-bill-would-force-teachers-to-out-lgbtq-students-to-parents/

Mandinach, E. B. (2012). A perfect time for data use: Using data-driven decision making to inform practice. *Educational Psychologist, 47*(2), 71–85.

Mandinach, E. B. (2017, April). *Data literacy for teachers: What it is, how do we make it happen, and implications for ETS*. Invited presentation at Educational Testing Service, Princeton, New Jersey.

Mandinach, E. B., Bocala, C., & Perrson, H. (2017). *Findings from the New Review of State Licensure Documents*. WestEd.

Mandinach, E. B., Friedman, J. M., & Gummer, E. S. (2015). How can schools of education help to build educators' capacity to use data: A systemic view of the issue. *Teachers College Record, 117*(4), 1–50. http://www.tcrecord.org/PrintContent.asp?ContentID=17850

Mandinach, E. B., & Gummer, E. S. (2011). *The complexities of integrating data-driven decision making into professional preparation in schools of education: It's harder than you think*. CNA Education, Education Northwest, and WestEd.

Mandinach, E. B., & Gummer, E. S. (2013). A systemic view of implementing data literacy into educator preparation. *Educational Researcher, 42*(1), 30–37.

Mandinach, E. B., & Gummer, E. S. (2016a, September). *Data and educator preparation programs: Data for programmatic continuous improvement and data literacy for teachers*. Keynote address at the annual CAEP conference, Washington, DC.

Mandinach, E. B., & Gummer, E. S. (2016b). *Data Literacy for Educators: Making it Count in Teacher Preparation and Practice.* Teachers College Press.

Mandinach, E. B., & Gummer, E. S. (2016c). What does it mean for teachers to be data literate: Laying out the skills, knowledge, and dispositions. *Teaching and Teacher Education, 60*, 366–376.

Mandinach, E. B., & Gummer, (Eds.). (2021). *The Ethical Use of Data in Education: Promoting Responsible Policies and Practices*. Teachers College Press.

Mandinach, E. B., & Jimerson, J. B. (2021). What does the future of data ethics look like? In E. B. Mandinach & E. S. Gummer (Eds.), *The Ethical Use of Data in Education: Promoting Responsible Policies and Practices* (pp. 233–245). Teachers College Press.

Mandinach, E. B., Jimerson, J. B., Siegl, J., & Tebbenkamp, M. (2023). *Student data privacy and data ethics scenarios for school leaders*. Future for Privacy Forum and WestEd. https://studentprivacycompass.org/wp-content/uploads/2023/07/Student-Data-Privacy-Scenarios.pdf

Mandinach, E. B., & Nunnaley, D. (2017). *Practitioner data literacy: Modules for teacher education*. WestEd.

Mandinach, E. B., & Nunnaley, D. (2021). The role of professional development providers in training data ethics. In E. B. Mandinach & E. S. Gummer (Eds.), *The Ethical Use of Data in Education: Promoting Responsible Policies and Practices* (pp. 144–172). Teachers College Press.

Mandinach, E. B., & Schildkamp, K. (2021). Misconceptions about data-based decision making in education: An exploration of the literature. *Studies in Educational Evaluation, 69*, 1–10.

Mandinach, E. B., & Warner, S. (2021, November). *Culturally responsive data literacy: The role of educator preparation*. Webinars given for the Branch Alliance.

Mandinach, E. B., & Warner, S. (2022, June). *Culturally responsive data literacy: What it is and how to reflect the concept in state standards*. Workshop given at the annual meeting of the National Association of State Directors of Teacher Education and Certification, Boston.

Mandinach, E. B., Warner, S., & Mundry, S. E. (2019, November). *Using data to promote culturally responsive teaching* (webinar). U.S. Department of Education, Institute of Education Sciences, National Center for Education Evaluation and Regional Assistance, Regional Educational Laboratory Northeast & Islands.

Mandinach, E. B., Warner, S., & Mundry, S. E. (2020, June). *Using data to promote culturally responsive teaching: Workshop 2* (webinar). U.S. Department of Education, Institute of Education Sciences, National Center for Education Evaluation and Regional Assistance, Regional Educational Laboratory Northeast & Islands. https://www.youtube.com/watch?v=2ZZuyFXpqZM

Mandinach, E. B., Warner, S., & Lacireno-Paquet, N. (2020, September). *Culturally responsive data literacy: Integration into practice in schools and districts* (webinar). U.S. Department of Education,

Institute of Education Sciences, National Center for Education Evaluation and Regional Assistance, Regional Educational Laboratory Mid-Atlantic.

Montini, E. J. (2023, March). Hey parents, flood Horne's hotline with positive calls. *Arizona Republic*. https://www.azcentral.com/story/opinion/op-ed/ej-montini/2023/03/16/flood-tom-horne-empower-hotline-critical-race-theory-positive-teachers/70016210007/

Mueller, J. (2023, March). Jodi Picoult doubles down against Florida book ban in new op-ed. *The Hill*. https://thehill.com/blogs/in-the-know/3898749-jodi-picoult-doubles-down-against-florida-book-bans-in-new-op-ed/

Muniz, J. (2019). *Culturally responsive teaching: A 50-state survey of teaching standards*. https://www.newamerica.org/education-policy/reports/culturally-responsive-teaching/

Muniz, J. (2020). *Culturally responsive teaching: A reflection guide*. https://d1y8sb8igg2f8e.cloudfront.net/documents/Culturally_Responsive_Teaching_A_Reflection_Guide_2021_WAMBwaO.pdf

National Association of State Directors of Teacher Education and Certification. (2021). Model Code of Ethics for Educators. https://www.nasdtec.net/page/MCEE_Doc

National Association of State Directors of Teacher Education and Certification. (2023). Model Code of Ethics for Educators. https://www.nasdtec.net/page/MCEE_Doc

National Forum on Education Statistics. (2024). *Forum Guide to Data Literacy* (NFES 2024-079). U.S. Department of Education, National Center for Education Statistics.

National Forum on Education Statistics. (n.d.). *Publications*. https://nces.ed.gov/forum/publications.asp

Nichols, S. L. (2021). Educational policy contexts and the (un)ethical use of data. In E. B. Mandinach & E. S. Gummer (Eds.), *The Ethical Use of Data in Education: Promoting Responsible Policies and Practices* (pp. 81–97). Teachers College Press.

Nichols, S. L., & Berliner, D. C. (2007). *Collateral Damage: How High-Stakes Testing Corrupts America's Schools*. Harvard Education Press.

Nickerson, R. S. (1998). Confirmation bias: A ubiquitous phenomenon in many guises. *Review of General Psychology, 2*(2), 175–220.

Nishioka, V. (2021, April). *Improving racial equity in school discipline through culturally responsive SEL*. REL Northwest. https://ies.ed.gov/ncee/edlabs/regions/northwest/blog/culturally-responsive-sel.asp

Obama, B. (2021, October 7). Arizona Speakers Series [speech transcript]. https://arizonaspeakersseries.com/

Paris, D. (2012). Culturally sustaining pedagogy: A needed change in stance, terminology, and practice. *Educational Researcher, 41*, 93–97.

Park, V. (2018). Leading data conversation moves: Toward data-informed leadership for equity and learning. *Educational Administration Quarterly, 54*(4), 617–647.

Paris, D., & Alim, H. S. (2014). What are we seeking to sustain through culturally sustaining pedagogy? A loving critique forward. *Harvard Educational Review, 84*(1), 85–100.

REL Mid-Atlantic. (2019, July). *Ask a REL question*. https://ies.ed.gov/ncee/edlabs/regions/midatlantic/askarel_106.asp

REL Midwest. (n.d.). *Measuring the use of culturally responsive practices*. https://ies.ed.gov/ncee/rel/infographics/pdf/REL_MW_Measuring_the_Use_of_Culturally_Responsive_Practices.pdf

REL Southwest. (2021). *Culturally responsive practices to support American Indian English learners' success* (infographic). https://ies.ed.gov/ncee/rel/Products/Region/southwest/Resource/100437

Safir, S., & Pugh, J. (2021). *Street Data: A Next-Generation Model for Equity, Pedagogy, and School Transformation*. Corwin.

Sangalang, J., & Wagner, J. (2023, March). James Patterson, Judy Blume, Toni Morrison, Jodi Picoult on list of 80 books one Florida school district pulled. *TCPalm*. https://www.tcpalm.com/story/news/2023/03/16/list-florida-school-district-removes-books-sex-racial-content-martin-county/70009140007/

Scheetz, M., & Senge, P. (n.d.). *Equity-centered capacity building: Essential approaches for excellence & sustainable school system transformation*. https://capacitybuildingnetwork.org/article3/

Shulman, L. S. (1986). Those who understand: Knowledge growth in teaching. *Educational Researcher, 15*(2), 4–14.

Shulman, L. S. (1987). Knowledge and teaching: Foundations of the new reform. *Harvard Educational Review, 57*(1), 1–22.

SLDS Support Team. (2017). *SLDS data use standards: Knowledge, skills, and professional behaviors for effective data use.* https://nces.ed.gov/programs/slds/pdf/datausestandards_knowledge_skills_professionalbehaviors.pdf

Stanford Center for Learning and Equity (SCALE). (2014). *edTPA.* https://www.edtpa.com/

Statewide Longitudinal Data Systems Grant Program. (n.d.). *About the SLDS Grant Program.* https://nces.ed.gov/programs/slds/about_SLDS.asp

Taylor, C. S. (2022). *Culturally and Socially Responsive Assessment: Theory, Research, and Practice.* Teachers College Press.

Walrond, N. (2021). *Serving the whole person: Alignment and coherence for local education agencies.* WestEd.

Walrond, N., & Romer, N. (2021). *Serving the whole person: Alignment and coherence for state education agencies.* WestEd.

Warner, S. (2021). *Culturally responsive data literacy.* WestEd, National Center for Systemic Improvement. https://ncsi-library.wested.org/resources/729

Venkateswaran, N., Feldman, J., Hawkins, S., Lewis, M. A., Armstrong-Brown, J., Comfort, M., Lowe, A., & Pineda, D. (2023). *Bringing an equity-centered framework to research: Transforming the researcher, research content, and practice of research.* RTI Press. https://www.rti.org/rti-press-publication/bringing-equity-centered-framework-research/fulltext.pdf

Vermont Agency of Education. (2021). *Vermont's education recovery: Framework and overview.* https://education.vermont.gov/sites/aoe/files/documents/edu-framework-vermonts-education-recovery.pdf

White House. (2021, January). *Executive order on advancing racial equity and support for underserved communities through the federal government.* https://www.whitehouse.gov/briefing-room/presidential-actions/2021/01/20/executive-order-advancing-racial-equity-and-support-for-underserved-communities-through-the-federal-government/

White House. (2023, March). *Fact sheet: White House Office of Science and Technology Policy announces progress on advancing equitable data.* https://www.whitehouse.gov/ostp/news-updates/2023/03/24/fact-sheet-white-house-office-of-science-and-technology-policy-announces-progress-on-advancing-equitable-data/

Index

accountability, 1, 2, 5, 14, 15–16, 22, 23, 96
assessment bias, 17, 20
assessment literacy, ix, 8, 10, 11, 22–23, 31
asset model, ix, 2, 5, 7, 9, 13, 14, 15, 16, 18, 19, 20, 23, 30, 33, 36, 39
attribution theory, 2, 5, 7, 13, 14, 16–17

bias, 3, 4, 5, 10, 14, 15, 16, 18, 19, 20, 21, 24, 26, 27, 28, 30, 31, 33, 35, 36, 37, 117, 118

confirmation bias, 5, 7, 14, 20, 37
conflation, assessment literacy and data literacy, 8, 22–23, 31, 119
consequences, intended and unintended, 2, 3, 4, 5, 12, 16, 20, 23
continuous improvement, 5, 7, 12, 14, 17, 20, 37
culturally responsive data literacy (CRDL), vii, viii, ix, 1, 2, 3, 4, 6, 7, 8, 9–14, 17, 18, 20, 22–24, 29, 30, 31, 32, 34, 35, 36, 37, 109, 110, 111, 112, 113, 114, 115, 117, 119, 120, 121, 122
culturally sustaining practice, 2, 6, 18–19, 32
cultural relevance, 2, 6, 18–19, 32
culturally responsive practice, vii, ix, 1, 2, 5, 6, 7, 14, 16, 18–19, 23, 29, 31, 32, 34

data-driven decision making, 1, 2, 8, 14, 16, 23, 33, 110, 118
data ethics, viii, 2, 5, 6, 10, 30, 33, 36, 37, 111, 112, 113, 118, 120
data literacy, vii, viii, ix, 1, 5, 6, 7, 8, 9, 11, 22, 23, 29, 30, 31, 32, 33, 34, 110, 111, 112, 113, 114, 117, 119, 120, 121

data literacy for teachers (DLFT), vii, viii, 1, 2, 3, 5, 6, 7–14, 21, 22, 23, 24, 29, 30, 31, 34, 110, 112, 113, 114, 117, 118, 119, 120
deficit thinking, 2, 5, 7, 9, 14, 15, 16, 17, 18, 20, 37, 117

educator preparation programs, ix, 3, 4, 7, 22, 31, 109, 113, 119, 120, 121
equity, vii, viii, ix, 2, 3, 5, 7, 14, 15, 16, 17, 18, 19, 20, 22, 23, 24, 32, 36, 37, 111, 113, 114, 117, 120, 121

guiding questions, 5, 6, 24–28, 35, 37

licensure and certification, viii, ix, 22, 31, 109, 112, 113, 114, 120
local education agencies, vii, 3, 6, 31, 33, 109, 110, 111–112, 120

professional development, 6, 7, 8, 16, 22, 29, 34, 36, 38, 109, 113–114, 120, 121
professional organizations, ix, 6,7, 8, 22, 29, 109, 112, 119–120

scenarios, 6, 28, 35, 38–108
scenarios, how to use and structure, 6, 28, 35–38
social justice, 18, 19, 20, 21, 23
standards, national and professional, 7, 22, 29–30, 31–32, 34, 36, 109, 111, 120
standards, state, ix, 6, 20–21, 23, 29, 31, 32–33, 109, 120
state education agencies, 6, 29, 31, 109, 110, 111, 112, 119, 120

street data, 19–20
student privacy, viii, 4, 10, 14, 30, 31, 33, 36
systems thinking, 2, 3, 6, 19, 109–115, 117

teacher knowledge, 3, 9, 21, 117, 120, 121

unconscious bias, 2, 3, 4, 5, 11, 12, 15, 19, 20, 26, 35, 37
U.S. Department of Education, 33, 109, 110–111

whole child, ix, 2, 5, 10, 13, 29, 30, 31, 33, 35, 36, 37, 111, 114, 117, 119, 120, 121

About the Author

Ellen B. Mandinach is a senior research scientist and a leading expert in data-driven decision-making at the classroom, district, and state levels. Her work over the past 20 years has focused on understanding how educators use data to inform practice. She has written and spoken widely on the topic and has served on a number of technical working groups and advisory boards on data use. She first developed the construct data literacy for teachers and now culturally responsive data literacy. Dr. Mandinach is working with schools of education, teacher preparation programs, professional organizations, and state and local education agencies to help them integrate CDRL and data ethics into their work. Most recently, she has been helping build the data infrastructure at the Nevada Department of Education and in districts throughout Vermont. She is developing materials on data privacy and data ethics for educator preparation and in-service training to help educators use data effectively and responsibly.

Dr. Mandinach has authored dozens of publications for academic journals, technical reports, and seven books. She has guest-edited several special issues of journals, including *Teachers College Record*, *Studies in Educational Evaluation*, and *Teaching and Teacher Education*. She was an author on the IES Practice Guide, *Using Student Achievement Data to Support Instructional Decision Making*. Recent books, *Data Literacy for Educators: Making It Count in Teacher Preparation and Practice* and *Transforming Teaching and Learning Through Data-Driven Decision Making*, are volumes that help educators to make better use of data. Her most recent book, *The Ethical Use of Data in Education: Promoting Responsible Policies and Practice*, focuses on data ethics in education. She has regularly presented at international, national, and regional conferences on education and psychology. She received the 2015 Paul D. Hood Award for Distinguished Contribution to the Field from WestEd. She has served as the president of the American Psychological Association's Division of Educational Psychology. She created the Data-Driven Decision Making in Education Special Interest Group of the American Educational Research Association and served as its first chair. She is a fellow of APA and AERA. She received an AB in psychology from Smith College and a PhD in educational psychology from Stanford University.

www.ingramcontent.com/pod-product-compliance
Lightning Source LLC
Chambersburg PA
CBHW080838230426
43665CB00021B/2881